LIVING WITH KINDNESS

SANGHARAKSHITA

LIVING WITH KINDNESS

THE BUDDHA'S TEACHING ON METTĀ

WINDHORSE PUBLICATIONS

Published by
Windhorse Publications
169 Mill Road
Cambridge
CB1 3AN, UK
email: info@windhorsepublications.com
web: www.windhorsepublications.com

First Edition 2004
Second Edition 2008
Reprinted 2012, 2014

Cover design by Marlene Eltschig
Cover image courtesy of Digital Vision / Robert Harding
Printed by Bell & Bain Ltd, Glasgow

British Library Cataloguing in Publication Data:
A catalogue record for this book is available from
the British Library

ISBN-10: 1 899579 64 8
ISBN-13: 978 1 899579 64 8

CONTENTS

ABOUT THE AUTHOR

Sangharakshita was born Dennis Lingwood in South London, in 1925. Largely self-educated, he developed an interest in the cultures and philosophies of the East early on, and realized that he was a Buddhist at the age of sixteen.

The Second World War took him, as a conscript, to India, where he stayed on to become the Buddhist monk Sangharakshita. After studying for some years under leading teachers from the major Buddhist traditions, he went on to teach and write extensively. He also played a key part in the revival of Buddhism in India, particularly through his work among followers of Dr B.R. Ambedkar.

After twenty years in India, he returned to England to establish the Friends of the Western Buddhist Order in 1967, and the Western Buddhist Order (called Trailokya Bauddha Mahasangha in India) in 1968. A translator between East and West, between the traditional world and the modern, between principles and practices, Sangharakshita's depth of experience and clear thinking have been appreciated throughout the world. He has always particularly emphasized the decisive significance of commitment in the spiritual life, the paramount value of spiritual friendship and community, the link between religion and art, and the need for a 'new society' supportive of spiritual aspirations and ideals.

Sangharakshita has now handed on most of his responsibilities to his senior disciples in the Order. From his base in Birmingham, he is now focusing on personal contact with people, and on his writing.

PREFACE

When the Dalai Lama was recently asked about the nature of his beliefs as a Buddhist he replied, 'My religion is kindness,' and there can be few Buddhists who would argue with that as a sound-bite definition of Buddhism. So how can this rather humdrum human response form the basis for a religious faith?

The quality he referred to as kindness is indeed central to all forms of Buddhism, but most Buddhists prefer to use the more precise and penetrating traditional term for it: *maitrī* (Sanskrit) or *mettā* (Pāli). What really distinguishes mettā from what we usually think of as basic human kindness is that mettā is a quality developed through practice, specifically the practice of the *mettā bhāvanā* meditation – the cultivation of universal loving kindness. As such, mettā is potentially boundless in its scope. There is no limit to how far you can take it.

At the same time, mettā is always rooted in that basic quality of ordinary human kindness. Just to reach out of one's self-absorption, however momentarily, and connect with the life around one, is to muster the basic ingredients one needs to perform this meditation. The cultivation of the inner life can become somewhat self-referential, if not alienating, without this practice, and as Sangharakshita emphasizes in the pages that follow, it is effective only if it translates back into ordinary human kindness.

Sangharakshita himself is certainly well qualified to talk about mettā, both in its theory and its practice. Throughout his life he has read widely, studied assiduously, and reflected deeply. At the same time, despite his personal inclination to a life of quiet reflection and study, he has always worked for the welfare of others, both in India, especially with Dr Ambedkar's mass conversion movement of ex-Untouchables in the 1950s, and in the West, with his founding of the Friends of the Western Buddhist Order.

It is always hard to pin a Buddhist down to anything like a credo. Sangharakshita would for example probably differ from the Dalai Lama on one or two issues. However, he long ago made a clear statement of his faith, in which he can be seen to follow very much the same spiritual impulse that the Dalai Lama would one day acknowledge as the key principle of his own life, encapsulated in the idea of mettā. In a booklet published in 1986 Sangharakshita writes:

I believe that humanity is basically one. I believe that it is possible for any human being to communicate with any other human being, to feel for any other human being, to be friends with any other human being. This is what I truly and deeply believe. This belief is part of my own experience. It is part of my own life. It is part of me. I cannot live without this belief, and I would rather die than give it up. For me, to live means to practise this belief.[1]

We have assembled this book mostly from the transcript of a seminar on the *Karaṇīya Metta Sutta* – the classic Buddhist text on the subject of mettā – led by Sangharakshita in July 1978 at Padmaloka retreat centre. As usual with books compiled from Sangharakshita's lectures and seminars, we have deliberately retained Sangharakshita's relaxed delivery in order to make a clear contrast with the literary finish of his written work. The reader should bear in mind that while Sangharakshita still checks and corrects the books that are published in this way, the result is nothing like a book he would have written on the subject himself. The emphases are inevitably determined by the seminar participants and their particular concerns. Equally inevitably, the discussion is more discursive than one would normally expect from a book written in the usual way.

However, it is probably true to say that Sangharakshita's boldest and most radical teaching is contained in his lectures and seminars. This is certainly where he has made his greatest impact on the lives of ordinary people, both in India and in the West. And there is always the added bonus of the anecdotes he draws from his colourful life or his very wide reading.

There are many English translations of the *Karaṇīya Metta Sutta* available today, including a poetic rendering by Sangharakshita himself. However, when the seminar was conducted, there were a limited number to choose from. F.L. Woodward had produced both a prose version and one in blank verse, and there was also a translation by Robert Chalmers in print. The one used in this seminar was by Saddhatissa. In common with Woodward's approach, Saddhatissa's language follows the usual custom of his time with regard to translations of Buddhist texts, in being archaic and dignified in its vocabulary and rhythms, without detracting from the simplicity and clarity of this beautiful sutta.

The editors are grateful to Vidyadevi, Khemavira, Dharmashura, and Leah Morin for invaluable assistance in moving this book towards publication.

Jinananda and Pabodhana
June 2004

KARAṆĪYA METTA SUTTA

He who is skilled in his good, who wishes to attain that state of calm (Nibbāna), should act thus: he should be able, upright, perfectly upright, of noble speech, gentle, and humble.

Contented, easily supported, with few duties, of light livelihood, with senses calmed, discreet, not impudent, not greedily attached to families.

He should not pursue the slightest thing for which other wise men might censure him. May all beings be happy and secure, may their hearts be wholesome!

Whatever living beings there be: feeble or strong, tall, stout or medium, short, small or large, without exception; seen or unseen, those dwelling far or near, those who are born or those who are to be born, may all beings be happy!

Let none deceive another, nor despise any person whatsoever in any place. Let him not wish any harm to another out of anger or ill will.

Just as a mother would protect her only child at the risk of her own life, even so, let him cultivate a boundless heart towards all beings.

Let his thoughts of boundless love pervade the whole world: above, below and across without any obstruction, without any hatred, without any enmity.

Whether he stands, walks, sits or lies down, as long as he is awake, he should develop this mindfulness. This they say is the noblest living here.

Not falling into wrong views, being virtuous and endowed with insight, by discarding attachment to sense desires, never again is he reborn.

Introduction

THE MEANING OF METTĀ

The great secret of morals is love; or a going out of our own nature, and an identification of ourselves with the beautiful which exists in thought, action, or person, not our own. A man, to be greatly good, must imagine intensely and comprehensively; he must put himself in the place of another and of many others; the pains and pleasures of his species must become his own.[2]

The question of happiness – or the problem of unhappiness – is fundamental to Buddhism. If we could be sure that we would never experience sorrow or disappointment, we would have no need of the Buddha's teaching. But, things being as they are, we need to find a way to deal with our human predicament. This is what the Buddha himself sought to do, and succeeded in doing. Having solved the problem himself, he spent the rest of his life explaining to others the nature of the solution and how it is to be achieved.

The Buddha's problem-solving approach finds expression in one of his most famous teachings, that of the four noble truths, a teaching which offers a kind of blueprint for Buddhist practice. The first of these truths states quite simply that unhappiness exists as a feature of human experience. This is to state the obvious, no doubt. But the second noble truth, the cause of suffering, gives more food for thought. The essential cause of suffering, the Buddha says, is craving, the natural but painful desire for things to be other than they are. If we can let go of that desire, if we can accept the rise and fall of experience as it is – not just in our heads, but in our heart of hearts – the problem of suffering will be solved.

Of course, this is far easier said than done. But it *can* be done. The third noble truth is the truth of Nirvāṇa, the truth that the end of suffering can be achieved, not through elevation to some heavenly state in some other place or time, but in this life, through one's own efforts to transform one's experience. What the Buddha is saying is that every human being has the capacity to become not just happy but Enlightened. The figure of the Buddha himself, the man Siddhārtha, whose own spiritual progress is charted in the texts of the Pali canon, is the enduring example of such self-determination. He embodied the sublime potential that can be activated in the human mind when it is turned resolutely towards the positive. The method of this transformation is outlined in the fourth of the noble truths, the noble eightfold path, each step of which, all the way to Enlightenment, is based on the truth of conditionality, the principle of cause and effect that underlies every aspect of the Buddhist approach to human growth and development. All things change, as we know to our sorrow, but this very fact becomes the source of joy when we realize that we ourselves have the power to change ourselves and our experience.

People sometimes prefer to think of Buddhism as a philosophy, or even a system of rational thought, rather than a religion. Buddhism does not, after all, rely upon divine aid as the means to happiness, but instead emphasizes the value of transforming one's experience in the light of a clear understanding of the nature of change. As such, it is a highly systematic teaching. But if we are not careful, we can end up thinking of the Buddha as a rather scholarly intellectual delivering lists of terms and definitions, an image which does justice neither to the depth of his wisdom, which goes far beyond words and terms, nor to the all-embracing breadth of his compassion. There are some forms of Buddhism in which a somewhat cerebral idea of the Buddha persists, and in which, consequently, little emphasis is placed on the emotional aspect of the Buddhist life. One might get the idea that we are supposed to keep our emotions firmly in check and concentrate on applying logic if we are to pursue insight into the nature of reality. There may even emerge a picture of the ideal

Buddhist as someone who has gone beyond any kind of emotion, as though all strong emotions were unspiritual, or even unethical, and this view does suit some people.

But a close look at the early Buddhist texts reveals a different picture. Throughout the ancient scriptures of the Pali canon it is made clear that the way to Enlightenment involves the cultivation of the emotions at every step, most often in the form of the four *brahma vihāras* (the Pali words can be translated as 'Sublime Abidings'). This series of meditations is designed to integrate and refine one's emotional experience so as to produce four different but closely related emotions: *mettā* or loving-kindness, *muditā* or sympathetic joy, *karuṇā* or compassion, and *upekkhā* or equanimity. *Mettā* is the foundation of the other three *brahma vihāras*; it is positive emotion in its purest, strongest form. In this book we will be exploring in detail the Buddha's account of how this positive emotion is to be cultivated, as laid out in a text called the *Karaṇīya Metta Sutta*. But first let us examine the term *mettā* itself a little more closely. Of course, an emotion cannot be conveyed fully by verbal explanation, though poetry sometimes comes close to doing so. Then we have the added complexity of translation, as there is no exact English equivalent of the Pali word *mettā*. But nonetheless, let us try to get at least a sense of the nature of this very special emotion.

AN ARDENT GOOD WILL

Any friendly feeling, any friendship, contains the kernel of mettā, a seed that is waiting to develop when we provide it with the right conditions.

The Pali word *mettā* (*maitrī* in Sanskrit) is related to *mitta* (Sanskrit: *mitra*), which means 'friend'. *Mettā* can thus be translated as friendliness or loving-kindness. Developed to its full intensity, mettā is a down-to-earth care and concern directed to all living beings equally, individually and without reservation. The unfailing sign of mettā is that you are deeply concerned for the well-being, happiness, and prosperity of the object of your mettā, be that a person, an animal, or any other being. When you feel mettā for someone, you want them to be not just happy, but deeply happy; you have an ardent desire for their true welfare, an undying enthusiasm for their growth and progress.

The friendliness of mettā doesn't necessarily involve actual friendship in the sense of a personal relationship with the person towards whom you are directing it. Mettā can remain simply an emotion; it doesn't need to become a relationship. Nevertheless, when you feel mettā, you will want to go out to other beings, to help them and express good will towards them in everyday, practical ways, and thus friendships can easily develop out of mettā. If two people develop mettā towards each other, their mettā is likely to blossom into a true friendship – a friendship with a difference. The same goes for an existing friendship into which an element of mettā is introduced. The mettā will tend to take the self-interest out of the friendship, so that it becomes something more than the cheery camaraderie or emotional dependency that is the basis of most ordinary friendships. Friendship infused with mettā becomes *kalyāṇa mitratā* – spiritual friendship – which flourishes not on the basis of what each party gets out of the relationship, but by virtue of the mutual desire for the other's well-being that flows unreservedly in both directions.

Thus there is no rigid distinction to be drawn between 'worldly' friendliness – or the worldly friendships that may come of it – and mettā. As we shall see, in its most highly developed form mettā is akin to insight into the very nature of things (insight with a capital i, as I sometimes say). But as a developing emotion it remains for a very long time more akin to ordinary friendliness. Mettā is friendliness as we know it, carried to a far higher pitch of intensity than we are used to. In fact, it is friendliness without any limit whatsoever. Mettā is present in the feeling you have for your friends, but it includes the intention continually to deepen and intensify whatever element of disinterested good will there is within it. Any friendly feeling, any friendship, contains the kernel of mettā, a seed that is waiting to develop when we provide it with the right conditions.

There is by definition something active about mettā. We call it a feeling, but it is more precisely described as an emotional response or volition rather than a feeling in the sense of a pleasant, unpleasant, or neutral sensation. (This distinction between a feeling and an emotion is a basic Buddhist teaching.) It includes the desire to act on our positive feelings, to do something practical to help the object of our mettā to be happy, to look after their welfare and encourage their growth and progress, so far as lies in our power. As well as friendliness, therefore, mettā includes the active, outgoing sense of good will or benevolence.

So why don't we translate mettā as love? Love, especially romantic or parental love, can have the intensity and strength to move mountains, and this vigorous concern is one of the most important characteristics of mettā. The problem with the word love is that it can be applied to almost anything that takes your fancy, including simple objects of appetite: you love your children or your boyfriend, but also the scent of orange blossom and many more things besides. Mettā, on the other hand, is directed only towards living beings.

Moreover, when it is based on appetite or possessiveness, love always has the potential to turn sour, because that appetite may be thwarted, that possession may be taken away. The feelings of jealousy or resentment that derive from romantic – that is to say, dependent – love can be more powerful than the most positive feelings of love in full bloom. Even parental love can turn bitter when it is felt to be unreciprocated – when one's child's ingratitude is 'sharper than a serpent's tooth', as Shakespeare's King Lear describes it.

AN ECSTATIC ENERGY
Mettā is blissful, ecstatic, a naturally expansive desire to brighten the whole world, the whole universe, and universes beyond that.

While being careful to differentiate mettā from all sorts of other emotions, we need not be so precious about it that we refine it out of existence. In the *Itivuttaka*, a collection of sayings from the Pali canon, there is a passage in which the Buddha says of mettā that 'it burns and shines and blazes forth',[3] suggesting that it is closer to incandescent passion than what we usually think of as 'spiritual' emotion. The English terms friendliness, loving-kindness, and good will don't come close to expressing this sort of intensity and expansive energy.

Indeed, the words we tend to use for the more spiritual emotions – that is, the more refined and positive ones – are usually understood in a rather weak sense. For example, the words refinement and purity, which refer to the quality of being free from impurities, and in that sense concentrated or power-ful, suggest quite the opposite – something effete and diluted. When it comes to the more positive spiritual emotions, words seem to fail us. By contrast, our words for harmful and unrefined emotions – hatred, anger, jealousy, fear, anguish, despair – make a much more vivid and powerful impression.

Mettā, as I have described it, may seem pure but rather cool, aloof, and distant – more like moonlight than sunshine. We tend to have the same sort of idea of angels. These celestial beings, for all their purity, usually come across as rather weak and lacking in energy by comparison with devils, who tend to be both physically and spiritually powerful and full of vigour. Rather like the angelic realm, mettā or 'loving-kindness' is for most people ultimately just not very interesting. This is because it is difficult to imagine developing positive emotion to anything like the degree of intensity of one's experience of the passions. We rarely experience purely positive emotion that is also strong; if we do experience any really intense emotion, there is usually an element of possessiveness or aversion or fear in it somewhere.

It is not easy to get rid of emotional negativity and develop the strong and vigorous positive emotion that is true mettā. To do so, we have somehow to bring to the refined and balanced emotion of universal good will the degree of energy and intensity of lower, coarser emotions. To begin with, we have to acknowledge that this goes against the grain. If we are to do justice to mettā as an ideal, we have to be realistic about the kind of strong emotion we actually experience. It may seem strange, but this is the basis upon which a higher emotional synthesis may be achieved.

In our desire to be near the object of our passion, in our need to possess it and our longing for it to be part of us, we experience the energy and intensity that will eventually characterize our experience of mettā. Similarly, when we achieve the object of our passion we may for a brief moment experience the blissful calm, the balance and harmony, that also characterize the genuine mettā state. Mettā brings together the contrasting emotional reactions of dynamic energy and calm repletion into a single quality of emotion, completely transforming them in the process. Although, when it is fully developed, mettā is a feeling of harmony, both in oneself and with all beings, it also has a fiery, full-blooded, even ecstatic quality. Ecstasy literally means a sense of standing outside oneself, and this is how mettā can feel: it is marked by such an intensity of positive emotion that, when purely felt, it can carry you outside yourself. Mettā is blissful, ecstatic, a naturally expansive desire to brighten the whole world, the whole universe, and universes beyond that.

A RATIONAL EMOTION
When we think of others the most reasonable response is that of mettā.

Mettā is clearly a good thing in itself. But there is another reason to practise it, apart from its obvious merits as a very positive state of mind. It makes clear sense in terms not only of subjective feeling, but also of objective fact. This is brought out very clearly by the philosopher John MacMurray. He distinguishes first of all between intellect and reason, designating reason as the higher, or integrated and integrating, faculty. Reason, he says, is that within us which is adequate to objective reality.[4] When reason, thus defined, enters into intellect, you have an intellectual understanding that is adequate or appropriate to the objective situation, to reality. This definition of reason comes very close to the Buddhist understanding of *prajñā*, or wisdom.

Next, he goes on to point out that reason may be applied not only to intellectual understanding, but also to emotion. A brief example should illustrate the point. If, when you see a small spider, you fly into a panic, jump up, and run to the other end of the room, this is an irrational reaction: the emotion is not appropriate to the object, because the spider is not really harmful. But when reason, as defined above, enters into emotion, your emotional responses will be adequate or appropriate to the objective situation, the real situation.

We can see mettā in the same way. Unlike emotions like mistrust, resentment, and fear, mettā is the appropriate and adequate response to other human beings when we meet or think of them. That is, mettā is a rational emotion. When we think of others the most reasonable response is that of mettā. We will wish all other beings happiness and freedom from fear, just as we wish ourselves these things. To understand that one is not so very different from any other human being, and that the world does not revolve around oneself, is an example of an intellectual understanding that is adequate to reality. To proceed from such a basis provides an appropriate foundation for our interactions with others.

Mettā is the norm or measure of our human response to others. This term 'norm' does not mean average or ordinary: it is closer in meaning to words like template or pattern or model. It is an ideal to which one seeks to conform. It is in this sense that Caroline Rhys Davids and other early western scholars of Buddhism sometimes translated Dhamma as 'the Norm'. For all its shortcomings, this translation does bring out the sense of the Buddha's teaching as being the template of the spiritual life. Likewise, in the true sense of the word normal, a normal human being is someone who accords with the norm for humanity, and a normal human response is the response to be expected from that positive, healthy, properly developed, balanced human being. Mettā is the response to be expected, as it were, from one human being encountering another. There has to be that fellow feeling if we are to experience our humanity to the full. It is what Confucius called *jen* or human-heartedness: the appreciation of our common humanity, and the behaviour or activity that is based on that feeling.

Mettā is an emotional response to others that is appropriate to reality, and to that extent it has the nature of insight. That insight is likely to be fairly mundane to begin with – insight with a small i, one might say – but eventually it can become Insight with a capital i: *prajñā* or wisdom in the full sense. In other words, through the development of mettā you can eventually transcend the subject–object duality – and this is the ultimate goal of the wisdom-seeker.

THE SUBLIME ABIDINGS

Mettā is the synthesis of reason and emotion, right view and skilful action, unobstructed spiritual vision and the bliss of a warm and expansive heart.

In cultivating mettā, we are trying to develop what one might call the higher emotions, that is, those emotions that provide us with a means of bringing together our everyday consciousness and something more purely spiritual. Without such a possibility we have no way of approaching either the higher ranges of meditative experience – called *dhyāna* – or Enlightenment itself. It is as though mettā in the sense of an ordinary positive emotion stands midway between the worldly and the spiritual. First, we have to develop mettā in ways we can understand – just ordinary friendliness – and from there we can begin to take our emotions to a far higher degree of intensity.

As should now be clear, mettā in the true sense is different from ordinary affection. It isn't really like the love and friendliness we are used to; it is much more positive and much more pure. It is easy to underestimate mettā and think of it as being rather cosy and undemanding. It is difficult, after all, to conceive what it is really like; only when you have felt it can you look back to your previous emotional experience and realize the difference. The same goes for each of the four brahma vihāras. When we begin to cultivate compassion, for example, we have to take whatever seed of it we can find within ourselves and help it to grow. As time goes by, our experience of it will deepen, and if our efforts to develop it are accompanied by a keen appetite for studying the Dharma and a willingness to bring our ideals into our everyday activity, we can come to experience a very pure, positive compassion which is quite different from what we usually understand by the term. In the same way the pure experience of sympathetic joy, muditā, is, because of its intensity, entirely different from the ordinary pleasure we might take in knowing that somebody else is doing well.

Upekkhā, equanimity, is a spiritual quality of a particularly elevated kind. There are traces of it in ordinary experience, perhaps in the tranquillity that can be found in nature, in the experience of standing alone in a forest when the air is still and the trees stand silently around you. But upekkhā goes far beyond even that kind of stillness; it has an intense, definite, even dynamic character of its own. And that is only to describe upekkhā in its mundane sense. The fully developed brahma vihāra is peacefulness of an indescribably subtle and intense kind. Infused as it is by insight, it is as though there is nothing but that peace. It is truly universal and utterly immovable. It is not just an absence of conflict; it has a magnitude and a solidity all of its own. Since it partakes of the nature of reality itself, no kind of disturbance can affect it in any way.

Through cultivating mettā you lay a strong foundation for the development of Insight. In other words, the more adequate to reality your emotional responses become, the closer you are to Insight. In the Mahāyāna this fully realized mettā is called *mahāmaitrī*. 'Mahā' means 'great' or 'higher', and *maitrī* is the Sanskrit equivalent of *mettā*, so this is mettā made great, made into its ultimate, Enlightened form. Mahāmaitrī represents a Buddha's or Bodhisattva's response to the reality of sentient beings, though that response is not quite emotion as we understand it. For one thing, it is suffused with a clear and rational awareness. Sentient beings are suffering, so what reason can there possibly be not to feel sympathy? How can I not feel compassion? How can I not try to help them?

In a completely healthy person feeling and thinking are virtu-
ally identical. You think and feel at the same time; there is no
gap. But in most people thought and feeling are distinct and
even alienated from each other. If our thinking is over-objective
to the point of being calculating, while our feeling is over-
subjective to the point of being sentimental, our inclination will
be to shrink from that over-objective thought back into that
over-subjective feeling.

D.H. Lawrence refers to the activity of thought as 'Man in his
wholeness wholly attending',[5] which brings out the integrated,
emotionally alive quality of the awareness we should aim for in
our intellectual life. William Blake describes the relationship
between reason and emotion in another way. Reason, he says, is
the bound or outward circumference of energy, the bounding or
limiting factor which is necessary if the expression of energy is
not to degenerate into formlessness and muddle.[6] So reason is
what gives emotion its form. Significantly, it is not imposed from
without by force, so as to cramp or constrict the emotion. It
grows with the emotion, enabling it to express itself and body
itself forth in beauty and truth.

Likewise, when we generate mettā and compassion, this
involves mental, rational activity, not just feeling. We deliber-
ately prepare the appropriate conditions from which we know
that the feeling will arise. For example, we call to mind images of
the people towards whom we want to direct love and happiness.
Mettā is the synthesis of reason and emotion, right view and
skilful action, unobstructed spiritual vision and the bliss of a
warm and expansive heart.

Perhaps the earliest and certainly one of the most outstanding
examples of the Buddha's teaching on mettā is to be found in
one of the earliest surviving scriptures of the Pali canon: the
Karaṇīya Metta Sutta. Scholars have determined that the collection of teachings called the Sutta-Nipāta, from which the

Karaṇīya Metta Sutta is drawn, is in large part an early scripture, but by no means entirely so, containing a good deal of comparatively late material. It has also been established that the brahma vihāras are not only early but also central teachings in the Buddha's dispensation.

The sutta occurs twice in the Pali canon, once in the *Sutta-Nipāta* as the *Metta Sutta*, and once in the *Khuddakapāṭha*, where it is given the title that has become its more popular name, the *Karaṇīya Metta Sutta*. The form of the sutta is not a prosaic discourse, but a series of stanzas composed in quantitative measure – that is, in lines of a fixed number of syllables. Perhaps we could even think of it as a poem inspired by an intense experience of mettā.

The text consists of just ten verses. To begin with, it refers to the goal to be pursued and the clear-sighted and healthy ambition that one needs to pursue it. It goes on to set out the general moral character required as a basis for the development of mettā. Following this, we are introduced to the specifics of how to practise the mettā bhāvanā meditation, with a suggestion in the seventh verse of the degree of intensity to be achieved in our experience of mettā. Finally, the sutta sets out the fruits of the training, indicating the close connection between the cultivation of mettā and the development of Insight into the nature of reality.

The translation we are using, which is just one of the very many that have been made, is by Saddhatissa. Before we look at it in detail, line by line, word by word, you could perhaps read it through to yourself a few times. As I said, the text is really a kind of poem and, as with the reading of all poetry, but especially such meaningful poetry, just reading it is a kind of meditation, the atmosphere of which should pervade all that follows.

Chapter One

THE WAY OF METTĀ

clear-sighted in its recognition of the impermanent nature of things. If you are a morally skilful person, you see the suffering and disappointment that arise from narrow and deluded self-interest, especially your own, and you try to act, speak, and think more in accordance with reality. It is axiomatic for Buddhism that the self we guard so jealously is really no more than an idea. More than that, Buddhism teaches that it is precisely our guarding of the self, and our habitual grasping at things to reinforce this fixed sense of who we are, that is the root cause of all our difficulty and suffering in life.

Unskilful states always seek to drive the wedge of self-interest between things, obstructing the flow of life with the thought of our own benefit or gain. Moral skilfulness on the other hand lies in the avoidance of harmful emotions like envy, hatred, and greed, and the cultivation of positive emotions such as mettā, together with clarity of vision (traditionally called right view). In skilful states of mind, we act out of an awareness of things. We are able to put ourselves in another person's shoes and attempt to understand their troubles and difficulties, as well as their ideals and aspirations. We feel happy at the happiness of others. We are patient when others annoy or threaten us. We are generous with our possessions, our time, and our energy. We are willing to be helpful in any way we can. Above all we think, speak, and act in ways that are intended to benefit the situation as a whole, rather than just to further our own aims.

To be skilled in one's good is to aim for states of consciousness that are free from the dead weight of self-interest and recrimination. It is to know also how to go about achieving those mental states. On such a basis one will begin to enjoy one's experience with a lighter touch and a more discriminating eye, in the knowledge that this approach will lead one towards one's ultimate goal, towards one's real benefit and happiness.

THE BUDDHA'S VOICE:
CONDITIONAL, NOT IMPERATIVE
The Buddha is not issuing commandments, but clarifying the implications of possible courses of action.

Karaṇīyam means literally 'let him do'. If someone wishes to attain that state of calm, let him do this. The sense here – conditional rather than imperative – is very characteristic of the Buddha's teaching and appears time after time in the Pali scriptures. The Buddha is not issuing commandments, but clarifying the implications of possible courses of action. If you wish to see a certain outcome, says the Buddha, you will need to act in a certain kind of way.

The conditional statement appeals to one's intelligence, whereas the categorical or imperative statement can be said to appeal only to a desire to be relieved of personal responsibility. The imperative mood suggests a haste, almost an impatience, to see someone act in a particular way. You might offer rewards for compliance with your orders or threaten sanctions for non-compliance, but you don't want to waste time on unnecessary explanation. The imperative mood is the voice of all authority figures, from military commanders to busy parents. It is the voice of Jehovah, the God of the Old Testament, with his ten commandments, his plagues of locusts and boils, his fires and his floods.

During my days in India, I was once staying in Poona with my friend Dr Mehta when a Seventh Day Adventist couple turned up to visit him. The husband was an enthusiastic proponent of his religion, and almost as soon as they were inside the door he started trying to bring about the doctor's conversion to their own faith. Dr Mehta was a man of considerable intelligence, and the Christian preacher's approach proved entirely inadequate to this task. Apparently incapable of offering an argument based on reason, he sought to rely upon the persuasive power of the Bible, a power which came in his view not from its capacity to provide rational argument, but simply from its claim to be the word of God. 'But don't you see?' he kept saying, 'Here is what the Bible says. God is speaking to us directly through this book.' And he held the book up for Dr Mehta to see, as though its very existence was sufficient to forestall any possible doubt. It was as if we were rather dense in not letting go of our rational objections. His argument, which was in effect, 'It must be true, because it is true,' was like the one offered by harassed parents everywhere: 'Because I say so.' Eventually, it fell to the preacher's wife, who seemed to understand the nature of reason better than he did, to tug his sleeve and say to him, 'But, dear, the gentleman doesn't believe in the Bible.'

The conditional statement, by contrast, expresses calm, patience, and a respect for the individual's responsibility to assess the situation for him- or herself and choose what course of action, if any, to take. As for the imperative statement, unless there is an emergency it suggests that the person issuing the directive has an axe to grind, an emotional investment in the outcome. The imperative statement always contains a veiled threat of sanction and for this reason we should always be wary of it. If someone is unwilling to clarify why they want you to do or think or believe something, it is possible that they do not themselves know what those reasons are, and that they do not want to examine them for fear of being left with doubts. Any impatience with rational objections on their part, any tendency towards anger when their will is obstructed, suggests it would be wise to question their motives.

By contrast, Buddhism teaches that there is nothing wrong with doubt, and Buddhists are encouraged to think things through and come to their own conclusions. We might be surprised by the calmness and equanimity of even the most unsophisticated Buddhist monk in a traditional Buddhist country on encountering someone who does not share his religious outlook. His easy-going attitude is not born of intellectual woolliness, doctrinal carelessness, or the kind of relativism that sees all views as ultimately the same. It comes from the fact that he doesn't take things personally. He will be very happy to explain something of the Buddhist outlook to you if it seems appropriate to do so, but he will not feel threatened if he learns that you follow a different faith. He may privately think that you are not quite on the right track, but he will not allow that view to disturb his equanimity and friendly attitude to you.

The Dharma, the Buddha's teaching, is an appeal to one's intelligence in the broadest sense, not to one's willingness to believe. You have to be able to understand, for example, the connection of unskilful actions and states of mind with suffering, and of skilful actions and states of mind with happiness. The Buddha himself is represented in the scriptures as saying, 'Whether Buddhas come or whether they do not come, one thing is fixed and sure: out of craving arises suffering.' This is something you can verify yourself, with reference to your own experience. Whether Buddhas come or whether they do not makes not the slightest difference.

The figure of the Buddha, although central to Buddhism from an historical and inspirational point of view, is not central in a doctrinal sense in the way that belief in the figure of Christ as the son of God is central to the Christian tradition. Buddhism is founded not upon the will or even the personality of the Buddha, but upon the Dharma, the teachings of the Buddha, and the truth to which these teachings are a guide, and which the Buddha himself reveres.

The Buddha does claim to have experienced for himself the truth of what he teaches, and this is the source of his spiritual authority. But that is all the authority he has. It has no claim on us unless we choose to submit to it. If you are truly to develop, you have to make up your own mind about whether or not your life is satisfactory. If it isn't, it is up to you to decide what to do about it.

Buddhists down the ages have glorified the Buddha, and have gone so far as to make him – in the Mahāyāna sūtras – a symbol of ultimate reality itself. But even when he is seen in this way, that achievement is still only what any human being is capable of achieving. Buddhists believe that any individual can become an enlightened human being if they only make the effort and follow in the footsteps of the Buddhas. In doing so, you follow not commands or orders but an example. You see what the Buddhas have done, and that it is the most skilful thing to do; that it has brought those human beings in the past to their ultimate well-being, and that it can do the same for you.

It is one thing to accept the authority of a teacher, or to decide to take on a precept or rule; it is quite another thing to be expected to obey commandments. Inherent in the use of the imperative – the commandment rather than the precept – is a sense of coercion, and where there is coercion there cannot be any spiritual teaching worthy of the name. The spiritual life is dedicated to the development of the individual, especially the development of awareness, of your own consciousness, your own sense of responsibility. How can you be forced to do that? It would be a contradiction in terms.

This is why the sutta says that 'he who is skilled in his good, who wishes to attain that state of calm (Nibbāna), should act thus'. If you are not skilled in your good and don't particularly feel the need to attain Nibbāna, all well and good; this teaching isn't for you. Although the Buddha might reason with you, he would not attempt to coerce you into doing something that you were unwilling to do. To deny someone their ordinary human freedom or to threaten or cajole them is not to communicate the

Dharma. A presentation of spiritual principles that appears to come from a position of power or coercive authority is not really true to those principles. It is a secular statement, not one that comes from a position of spiritual authority.

So the conditional or hypothetical statement is the most appropriate way to communicate the Dharma. If the Buddha is the Śāntināyaka, the one who leads beings to peace, this is in a sense all he does, perhaps all he is capable of doing. Nobody is threatening you with hellfire and brimstone if you decide you are quite happy as you are. The Buddha simply shows the way. It is up to you to decide whether or not you want to follow it.

Chapter Two

THE
ETHICAL FOUNDATIONS
OF METTĀ

He should be able, upright, perfectly upright, of noble speech, gentle, and humble.

Sakko ujū ca sūjū ca
suvaco c'assa mudu anatimānī

The Buddha's conditional statement – that if you want this, you will need to do that – is more than an invitation, it is also a challenge. How ready are we to follow the path of peace? In the opening lines of the sutta we are introduced to the level that our ordinary human development needs to have reached if we are to embark on the path of the higher evolution, as I call it – that is to say, the path of conscious self-development by which we can realize our full spiritual potential. Leaving aside the spiritual qualities needed for this, do we have even the basic human qualities that such an undertaking calls for? At this stage, before attempting to develop the ideal response to others that we call mettā, we need to clarify how we relate to others at a basic level, perhaps by becoming more straightforwardly ethical. Until we have done this, our ideas about mettā will bear little or no relation to our ability to bring it into being in our everyday experience. Having told us what the 'one skilled in his good' is really aiming for, the sutta's first verse therefore goes on to tell us how such a person should act, not specifically but in general.

CAPABLE

The sutta is not looking for signs of incipient piety. It is not saying that you need to be a sensitive soul or a spiritual person. It is simply saying that you need to be capable.

It is worth noting that the first quality mentioned is one that most people would never think of associating with the spiritual life at all. *Sakko*, the word translated here as 'able', means just that: 'able to do', vigorous and adept. It suggests that the Buddhist approach to the spiritual life is quite practical and matter-of-fact. The sutta is not looking for signs of incipient piety. It is not saying that you need to be a sensitive soul or a spiritual person. It is simply saying that you need to be capable.

An example from the Pali canon shows us that some of the Buddha's very earliest disciples were anything but pious, at least to begin with. These young men were what one might today call playboys, looking for a good time and experiencing a measure of frustration and disillusionment in the process. They came from wealthy merchant families and, so the story goes, they were out picnicking one day in the countryside. They had all brought their wives along with them – all except one young man who had no wife but who had brought along a courtesan. This young woman then rather spoiled the outing for everyone by disappearing with some ornaments, and when the Buddha came across them they were busy searching for her.

Having set out to enjoy themselves, it all turned rather sour, and the Buddha seized this moment of disillusionment to suggest to the young men that there was a more reliable source of enjoyment to be found in the Dharma. Why waste your time searching for this woman, asked the Buddha, when it could be put to better use searching for yourself? Eventually, inspired by the Buddha's teaching, these playboys became what we would nowadays call monks.[8]

The episode has much that is worthy of reflection, but the point to be noted in this context is that these men were not obvious candidates for the spiritual life. They were not the types to be especially interested in religion or meditation. However, they were clearly able to know their own good, and to know what was even better when it was pointed out to them. They were psychologically sound, able to look after themselves, capable.

A person who is truly capable can turn their capability in almost any direction. You can go out to work or choose not to. You might know how to do a bit of gardening, you might know how to do a bit of carpentry, you might be able to look after a baby, or cook a meal from any leftovers in the kitchen. In fact, confronted with any given situation, difficult or otherwise, you can cope, you can manage, you can get by. You know how to look after yourself, and you can look after others if need be. This is the capable human being, the product of the long march of evolution, and the kind of person one will need to be in order to embark on the path of spiritual development. It doesn't matter whether or not you are interested in religion, philosophy, spirituality, mysticism, high art, or even Buddhism itself. None of this counts for much if you are not first of all a capable human being, someone who is able to be an effective member of society in the ordinary sense, to look after themselves, manage their own life, and make their own way in the world.

It should be said that being capable is not always a matter of one's own efforts alone. Some qualities are the result of all sorts of deep-seated conditions that stretch back through your life or that may simply be inherited. If you have had a supportive up-bringing – that is, one in which you have been surrounded by people who care about you, who have helped you grow and learn effectively – the necessary qualities may come to you quite easily, especially if, because of your personality, you have been able to make full use of these opportunities. In all likelihood you will have the resourcefulness and stability of mind to begin the path of self-directed spiritual practice.

Without these advantages you may find it hard to muster the ordinary human capability to take you forward in the spiritual life. If your upbringing and life experience has been particularly difficult, if there are psychological or emotional factors that stand in the way of spiritual progress, you may need time to overcome these and to integrate the various aspects of your personality into a single-minded clarity of purpose. You may be inspired by the Dharma but lack the practical human qualities and the mental toughness necessary to make a success of practising it. If you realize that you are psychologically frail or emotionally dependent, the best thing to do to begin with is to work steadily at that level. Not everybody who comes along to a Buddhist meditation class possesses the self-assurance, self-motivation, and independence of mind which are not only associated with successful human endeavour, but which also give the necessary drive to spiritual practice. If you are in this position you will have to devote your energies first to building up your basic psychological strength. You may benefit from therapy or analysis, but it may be even more helpful to work on your friendships and to learn to do a job competently and reliably.

Spiritual teachers have a responsibility not to push their students into a more demanding spiritual practice than they are ready for, or allow their students' enthusiasm to lure them into biting off more than they can chew. Meditation can help to sort out one's problems at this straightforward psychological level, just by introducing a little peace of mind, while ritual and devotion help to generate more energy and positivity. Retreats can deepen and stabilize one's practice. But even someone who meditates regularly and is definitely getting something from it will not necessarily be capable in the sense of remaining emotionally positive through all the ups and downs of a life dedicated to spiritual practice. Not everyone can form a resolution to act in a certain way and stick to it, for example. Becoming a healthy, capable human being takes time. I myself know people who have been meditating regularly for many years but who do not seem to have got very far spiritually. In some cases work and friendship are more effective ways of building up self-confidence and an ability to engage effectively with the world.

The sutta makes it quite clear that one has to be capable to begin with. Being capable is nothing extraordinary. It doesn't mean being perfect or infallible. It means being adequate, competent, able to make a reasonable success of your work. As such, it may seem a small thing. But being capable may not be something you can achieve immediately. If you do come to see that you are *not* yet capable in this way, this need not stop you from further spiritual endeavour. There are plenty of other qualities that may be more accessible, and the sutta goes on to tell us what they are.

UPRIGHT

If you habitually mask your true feelings out of fear of confronting people with the truth of yourself as you really are, you are hardly likely to be able to confront that truth yourself.

As well as being able, the one skilled in his good needs to be 'upright'. The Pali word is *uju*, a term which does not specifically refer to ethics but is more commonly associated with archery, being used to refer to the shaft of an arrow. It means quite simply 'straight'. Just as the shaft of an arrow needs to be straight if it is to hit its target, the followers of the Dharma need to be straight in order to be true to their aim. This quality of being upright or straight typically shows itself in our dealings with other people. It concerns the social sphere, the sphere of economic relations, and daily work.

In a sense, it follows on naturally from the first quality, being capable. There is a certain clean practicality in the attitude of one who is straight. If you are capable, you will do things in a straightforward, open, uncomplicated way. You don't need to resort to anything underhand or devious. You don't need to duck your responsibilities. You know what you think and you are honest in communicating it, without playing games or hiding behind half-truths. You are upright.

Being straightforward is often the key ingredient in Buddhist practice. It is so easy to compromise, to equivocate, to fudge the truth and dilute your intention. 'On the whole I'm pretty honest,' you might say, 'so there surely can't be any harm in softening the harsh reality a bit, covering up the raw truth, bending the bare facts a little, just to help things along.' It is true that equivocation can sometimes appear to prevent upset, at least in the short term, and avoid hurting people's feelings – even if your *own* feelings are the ones you are most concerned to protect. There is also no doubt that being straightforward can land you in trouble, and in business dealings it can create complications. Even from a worldly point of view, however, these difficulties will in most cases be offset in the longer term by a positive dividend of trust and respect from colleagues and clients.

From a spiritual point of view, we have to consider what the avoidance of confronting people or situations is really about. If you are watering down the truth of what is really going on, you are watering down your ability to apply the Dharma to your life. If you habitually mask your true feelings out of fear of confronting people with the truth of yourself as you really are, you are hardly likely to be able to confront that truth yourself. You need to be able to see the real danger in being woolly and vague, to see that avoiding the truth of the immediate situation fatally undermines your practice of the Dharma. Being upright in this context involves being clear about your aims and honest about how they are to be achieved.

The upright and straightforward person knows his or her own mind and is not afraid to speak it. Freedom from fear and anxiety is a natural consequence of this willingness to be honest. If you are genuinely straightforward, you will not attempt to conceal whatever negative emotions might arise. Even if you are prone to anger or lust or fear, you can acknowledge these tendencies, and so avoid the guilt and alienation that go with dissimulation and pretence. You will be emotionally engaged, self-confident, and uninhibited. The sutta is itself unequivocal and uncompromising in advocating this virtue: 'He should be able, upright, perfectly upright.' The only way to be straight, the sutta seems to be saying, is to be perfectly straight, straight without any qualification or rationalizing: *sūju*, 'perfectly and happily upright'. Let there be no doubt about it.

It might seem from this that being straightforward is a very straightforward virtue. However, one needs quite a degree of psychological integration if one is to have the kind of emotionally positive, trusting nature that can deal with others without feeling the need to obfuscate, dither, or beat about the bush. On the other hand, you may think you have no problem with being straightforward when in fact your plain speaking is close to boorishness. There is a difference between being open and candid and being simply blunt and crude. Harshness of speech can masquerade as honesty and openness when it really expresses a closed attitude towards others, a lack of awareness of the effect upon them of one's speech and manner. Some people pride themselves on being outspoken – 'I speak as I find' – when really it's just an excuse for being insensitive to other people's feelings. A straight approach can turn into a bludgeon if it goes with a lack of awareness of the complex differences in people's sensitivities, and an assumption that the consequences of your straight talking are not your affair.

So a further human quality that the sutta recommends to one who wishes to attain the state of peace is that of gracious speech, speech that is good, appropriate, and pleasant. We cannot afford to be abrupt or uncaring in our communication with others if we want to make progress towards that ultimate goal.

FLEXIBLE
Buddhism calls not for cringing self-abnegation,
but for heroic altruism.

A quality that offsets the unhelpful connotations of straight-forwardness or perfect uprightness in speech is *c'assa*, a word that seems to have caused translators a few problems. *C'assa* can be translated as 'obedient', but it is not exactly docility or submissiveness. It is more an amenability, a willingness to go along with other people's ideas as long as they are not actually unreasonable or misguided.

Amenability counteracts the obstinacy that tends to go with a straightforward attitude. Being amenable doesn't mean that you immediately allow others to have their own way against your better judgement. But you won't set your face against their sug-gestions just because those ideas were not originally your own. You are reasonable in debate and easy-going, especially in mat-ters of no great importance. And you will be prepared to follow the lead of someone more experienced or better qualified than you are.

The dictionary translation of the next adjective in this line, *mudu*, is 'soft, mild, weak, and tender'. Clearly, we can rule out 'weak' in the present context. We are left with a sweet temper, a mild and gentle manner, a tender responsiveness. It is a quality that emerges naturally out of the previous one: *mudu* suggests a pliancy, a suppleness of mind, without any sense of being weak or easily led. There is plenty of elasticity, plenty of 'give' in your attitude. Where flexibility is required, you can be flexible. You can adjust. You are adaptable and even-tempered.

Finally, there is *anatimānī*. It is translated here as 'humble', a word which carries some rather unfortunate connotations. Someone who is 'skilled in their good' is not going to adopt the obsequious, hand-wringing posture of one of Charles Dickens' more repellent characters, Uriah Heep, who repeatedly declares himself to be 'ever so 'umble'. Buddhism calls not for cringing self-abnegation, but for heroic altruism. *Māna* means 'mind', and *anati* 'not high' or 'not extreme', so *anatimānī* means an absence of high-and-mightiness, arrogance, or conceit. It does not preclude a proper pride or self-respect.

We now have a composite picture of one 'skilled in his good'. Such a person is capable, completely straightforward, gracious in their speech, amenable, flexible, and lacking any conceit. What is perhaps most significant about this initial impression of someone who is proficient in the means of attaining the state of peace is that if you were to meet such a person they would not necessarily strike you as religious, certainly not as pious or holy. These are simply positive human qualities. The sutta seems to be saying that the practice of Buddhism consists, first and foremost, in the conscious development of the ordinary virtues of the happy human being.

Contented, easily supported, with few duties,
of light livelihood, with senses calmed, discreet,
not impudent, not greedily attached to families.

Santussako ca subharo ca
appakicco ca sallahukavutti
santindriyo ca nipako ca
appagabbho kulesu ananugiddho

45

CONTENTED
*One's contentment, or lack of it,
is basically always with oneself.*

Santussako, or contentment, the first-mentioned quality of the
second verse, presupposes a degree of individuality. Firstly, the
contented person knows how to find satisfaction with what they
have. Of course, only a Buddha or Bodhisattva or Arhant would
be content in absolutely any situation, but in most circumstances
a contented person will have an inner peace, a brightness or
warmth or harmony within, that tends to obviate the need for
stimulation from outside. The person who is contented is thus
one who leads a simple life; conversely, one who leads a simple
life will become contented. Contentment is linked to individuality in that if you are an individual, you don't need anything special to compensate for some lack within yourself. You have a
being of your own; you are not unreasonably dependent on
external circumstances or on the approval of others. You find a
certain sufficiency or fulfilment within yourself, in the experience of your own being. It is in this sense that you are contented.

But in trying to be self-sufficient, and choosing not to expose
yourself to much in the way of stimulation or excitement, aren't
you shutting yourself off from others and closing your mind to
life in general? In fact, contentment is the opposite of a closed or
fixed state of mind. It is a state of openness and freedom. Contentment is a generous state of being wherein you have no need
to cling to anything, or gain anything, in order to be happy.
When you are content you have a healthy enjoyment of your
state of being, free from caginess or undue reserve.

Depending on your inner resources does not mean cutting
yourself off from other people. That would suggest not so much
contentment as complacency. As the near enemy of contentment, complacency betokens a superficial satisfaction with

things as they are, particularly with yourself. If you scratch the surface of this self-satisfaction, you are likely to find blind attachment to your present state at almost any cost. You inwardly – and perhaps not so inwardly – congratulate yourself on being the way you are, with no thought of ever becoming anything different, anything more. You regard your present state as final. You do not look beyond it, and underneath you are clinging to it for dear life.

Complacency is related to a fault referred to more directly in the first verse of the sutta: *atimānī*, or arrogance. The arrogant person, like the complacent person, does not want to go too deeply into anything that might threaten their fixed idea of who they are. Yet, ironically, complacency and arrogance stem from a lack of contentment with who you *really* are. Your apparent contentment is with who you *think* you are. You know – or you feel – that the real you is simply inadequate. Perhaps you are unwilling even to get to know the real you, and to explore your real identity, for fear of the shortcomings and inadequacies you may find. So instead, you climb on to your high horse and create a false self in place of the real self.

If you do that, you fend off any real communication, because true communication always involves opening yourself to others. An arrogant or complacent person would rather not know the truth about themselves, which in turn means that they cannot really be receptive to others. Only by learning to feel mettā for themself and others can such a person move on from their fixed, and therefore false, view of themself.

Stillness, simplicity, and contentment can be said to be the positive counterpart of the third precept, abstention from sexual misconduct. Without contentment, for example, a married person will perhaps experience dissatisfaction with their situation and start to look around for a new sexual partner. But when you are emotionally more self-sufficient – that is to say, more contented – you are aware that a sexual relationship cannot bring complete fulfilment, but only a certain level of satisfaction. You will then be more likely to be able to keep to the terms of the marriage contract, not looking outside it for some special experience that seems to promise greater fulfilment. You realize that contentment is found in what you are and what you have, not in what you could be and what you might have.

Our desire for the things we crave seldom bears any relation to the capacity of those things to satisfy that craving. People usually eat sweets not because of their flavour but for the temporary experience of reassurance they give. But reassurance is intangible, and certainly not to be found in a plastic wrapper, so we are more or less certain to be disappointed. Then, having failed to assuage our craving for reassurance, and in the absence of any more creative option, we are likely just to eat another sweet. It is as if we suffer from some constant niggling need, some nameless lack, some ever-present void that we try to fill with something, anything – a sweet, a special treat, a flick through the pages of a magazine or the television channels. This is the repetitive nature of neurotic craving. We cannot enjoy what seem to be the things we desire because what we really want is insubstantial. Although we see it in the object, it is not really there. The sweet, after all, does not contain reassurance; it only contains sugar. Reassurance is a subjective experience, and one can only find it by looking inwards.

One's contentment, or lack of it, is basically always with oneself. All our attempts to get satisfaction from external objects, all the hankering and scheming and yearning, come from this restlessness, this refusal to accept ourselves and our condition. If we are to become contented, therefore, there will need to be a radical shift of direction in our search for satisfaction. Trying to arrange the world to suit our desires will never produce the stillness and simplicity that characterize true contentment, but only the irritation and disappointment that come from dependence upon external conditions. Contentment can come only from our inner resources, from creating the appropriate conditions within our own mind. We are dissatisfied with our experience, but we look in the wrong place for the solution. We look out into the world for the remedy, in the form of desired objects and people, when we really need to be looking inwards, into the hidden treasure of the mind itself. To be contented, then, you need to have a positive appreciation of yourself. This is why the mettā bhāvanā meditation practice begins with the cultivation of mettā towards oneself. So you need to have a degree of contentment to practise the mettā bhāvanā, but then the practice itself will strengthen that sense of contentment.

We can begin to see that the practice of the mettā bhāvanā meditation can be an example of what is sometimes known in the Buddhist tradition as the path of irregular steps. According to the sutta, we need to have all these human qualities if we are to be able to feel and express mettā fully and effectively; but we will be greatly assisted in the development of qualities like contentment by our attempts to develop loving-kindness towards ourselves and others.

EASILY SUPPORTED
We need productive activity for our physical and psychological well-being.

In the first verse, the sutta sets out the qualities of the healthy human, one who is able to take responsibility for making their own way in the world. The second verse brings a transition, suggesting a more specifically mendicant lifestyle. The term *subharo*, 'easy to support', refers to the economic situation of the monk. The suggestion seems to be that we renounce work and commit ourselves to a life of contemplation, relying on the support of others to give us the necessities of life. The quality we have just been discussing, contentment, clearly also supports this. If they are not contented within themselves, the monk and nun will not be able to sustain their chosen lifestyles.

The fact is that in the Buddha's time, the monks were completely dependent upon lay people, who provided them with food, clothing, and even sometimes with shelter. With the basic necessities of life taken care of, the monks and nuns were free to devote their energies to meditation, study, and devotional practice. This being the case, it was the responsibility of the monks to be easy to support, and not to make life difficult for those who were considerate enough to provide them with their material needs.

The tradition of the homeless wanderer being supported by society at large was not instituted by the Buddha; he inherited it, it existed in Indian society already. In the Buddha's day, the renunciation of social identity was a common and accepted practice all over northern India, and the homeless wanderer or *paribbājaka* was thus an accepted outsider. When the Buddha started out on his journey to Enlightenment, he too left the home life to become a *paribbājaka*. After the Enlightenment many of his disciples came from that same casteless social category, or rather non-category, and continued to go on foot from village to village with their alms bowls, accepting whatever food they were given. In the early days of the Buddhist community, the *sangha*, the priority was to establish a spiritual community on principles that transcended the worldly concerns of the wider society. As the figure of the itinerant spiritual practitioner was already a feature of Indian society and the support of such individuals by the wider community an accepted tradition, the Buddhist sangha adopted this model quite naturally.

The withdrawal of the monk or nun from the world of work went with an attitude to work, particularly manual labour, which still persists in Indian society today: the view that it is inherently unspiritual. The ancient Indians had a similar view to that of the ancient Greeks except that, whereas the Athenian state relied on a class of slaves to carry out any manual labour that might be necessary, Indian society depended on a number of lower castes. The Greeks have of course given up slavery, but to a large extent India continues to run on the basis that physical work is inherently degrading, and that no respectable person would do such work if he or she could possibly avoid it.

Thus in the India of the Buddha's day the possibility of taking up the spiritual life and continuing to do physical work simply did not arise. You could not be a full-time spiritual practitioner and continue to support yourself. But by virtue of the same attitude, you could rely on the lay people to support you. Indeed, the religious renunciant was almost compelled to depend for alms on the lay community if he was to form any kind of socially acceptable relationship with them. Nor did the Buddha think it worth challenging this convention. It is not after all such a bad thing in principle for the more spiritually committed to be supported by the less committed. He accepted the customary division between monks or wanderers and lay communities as a reasonable way to make this happen, and a way of propagating the Dharma in the process. But as Buddhism developed and spread, the range of activities that the full-timers were able to take up expanded. In the beginning, they were expected to devote all their energies to meditation, study, and teaching. For the first 500 years the teaching was passed on entirely through oral transmission, so a good deal of the time would have been spent learning the suttas by heart and chanting them communally to impress the doctrine on the memory of every monk. Then, when the suttas began to be written down, a great deal of literary activity ensued. Later still, with the building of the great monasteries, monks would have been involved in the sculpting and gilding of images, as well as in the design and decoration of the monasteries and temples themselves.

Later, when Buddhism, especially in its Mahāyāna form, travelled to China and Tibet, whose cultures had a more practical inclination than that of India, monks began to take up everyday physical tasks. Tibet, for example, has no cultural prejudice against manual labour, and in a Tibetan Buddhist monastery you will find monks energetically engaged in all manner of necessary activities according to their various abilities. In the Ch'an and Zen schools, work is considered to be an integral part of a fully committed spiritual training. As in Tibetan monasteries, monks are expected to throw themselves wholeheartedly into every task that needs to be done, from cooking, cleaning, chopping wood, and drawing water to the printing of Buddhist texts.

So we have to be careful not to be trapped by our respect for ancient texts such as the *Karaṇīya Metta Sutta* into thinking of practical, physical, and even economic activity as being necessarily worldly or unspiritual. A human being is not only a mind, but also a body inhabiting a sensory, physical universe. We need productive activity for our physical and psychological well-being. If our mind is the only part of us that gets any real exercise, whether through study or teaching, or at an office desk or computer, there will be an imbalance in our being as a whole, and we will be in need of physical work and exercise to bring it back into balance.

I know from my own contact with Buddhist monks in Southeast Asia (admittedly as far back as the 1950s) that they can get into quite an unhealthy state – not just physically or psychologically, but also spiritually – from lack of exercise. Their dependence upon the laity, who in most cases looked after them extremely well, was such that even though the monks would have liked to have done more for themselves, the lay people would not let them. As I remember it, the lay people felt embarrassed, or even affronted, if the monks tried to do things for themselves. It is after all through service to the monks that lay people traditionally express their devotion to the ideal of Enlightenment.

On the face of it, the dependence of the full-time spiritual practitioners on the laity ought to contribute to the simplicity of their lifestyle, enabling them to concentrate more of their energy on purely spiritual matters. But in reality it can hinder them from engaging their energies at all. Perhaps in the early days of Buddhism this unequal distribution of labour between monks and laity was necessary. The dawn-to-dusk burden of physical labour was no doubt so heavy that a degree of freedom from such duties was essential if one was to have the time and energy for reflection and other higher pursuits. It is understandable that a conflict emerged between the demands of farm and field on the one hand and those of spiritual pursuits on the other, and an outright separation of the two was probably the most straightforward solution. However, the cost was a certain alienation: from worldly affairs on the part of the monks, and from any real spiritual life on the part of the laity.

It would seem then that this concept of *subharo*, 'easy to support', owes its appearance here to the social conventions prevalent in India at the time of the Buddha. In view of this it would be a mistake to interpret the term as suggesting that someone committed to leading the spiritual life must be materially supported by others, and should not get involved in practical or economic activity. In the market economies of the modern world, we are very fortunate in being able to be full-time Buddhists while at the same time involving ourselves unashamedly in straightforward, practical tasks. We should take that opportunity. In our practice of the Dharma there is invariably a healthy tension between the need to be involved in the sphere of worldly human activity, and thus practise the other-regarding aspect of the Dharma, and the need to withdraw from worldly activity for the purposes of meditation and reflection. As modern Buddhists we have a unique opportunity to decide for ourselves how this balance may be struck in our lives. In doing so, we need to return to the basic principles of Buddhism, and specifically to the principle of right livelihood, that is, ethical work.

To practise right livelihood, we may have to question our overall attitude to work. Like ancient cultures, industrialized societies have their own conventional attitudes to work, these attitudes being based in the case of the latter on the strict division between paid work and leisure. For many of us, work is an activity we don't *want* to do but *have* to do in order to support ourselves, and leisure time is 'our own time', in which we are free to pursue our personal interests. This unhappy distinction seems to affect much that we do. Jobs, tasks, physical activities with some practical purpose or end in view, like cleaning or cooking, are considered a burden, a chore, and resented as such; and we imagine that when we are not working we should be continuously diverted. We certainly don't want to have to do 'chores'.

However, all human beings, even spiritual full-timers, need work, in the sense of some productive, useful activity, whether paid or unpaid, that is beneficial to themselves and to others; and simple, practical physical work may be better than intellectual work from the point of view of fulfilling this human and spiritual need. If you are able to devote all your time and energy to meditation, study, teaching, and writing, all well and good. But not everyone is able to meditate or study the Dharma day in, day out. Many people, including many monks, are quite unsuited to teaching or writing. So, for them, an injunction to refrain from working and physical activity would be quite unhelpful. Of course, this means that we have to be able to carry out such work without resentment, without considering it demeaning or a burdensome imposition.

Today we have the opportunity to reappraise the whole question of work and financial support. We do not necessarily have to accept the traditions as they have come down to us, especially when these are influenced by Indian social and cultural conditions of some 2,500 years ago. In modern post-traditional societies, you can renounce family life and worldly occupation without having to rely for your livelihood on those who have chosen to engage with them. You can choose to work with other Buddhists – that is, others who share your aspirations – in such a way as to support one another's spiritual development and at the same time provide for the material needs of each one of you. The necessity to support oneself financially can become an opportunity to deepen communication, share skills, and learn new ways of cooperation and mutual support. Working in such a situation you can take full account of individual temperaments and attitudes to allow each person to work in a way that is appropriate to their spiritual needs. Some people might find it suits them best to do mainly manual work, while others would benefit from gradually taking on more managerial responsibility. Of course, everyone would need to have time for meditation and Dharma study.

In today's world, it is up to the individual to choose their own way, to make their own decisions, according to whatever principles they wish to live by. There can no longer be blanket rules for spiritual life and practice. What is appropriate at one time and in one place may not work in another. We need a new kind of Buddhist culture in which economic relations can be constantly recreated to meet a constantly changing world. This is probably as close to the Mahāyāna ideal of the Pure Land – the perfect environment for spiritual practice – as we can hope for.

GIVE WHAT YOU CAN, TAKE WHAT YOU NEED

There are very few people who would benefit spiritually from being entirely supported by others in the way that the traditional monastic sangha was.

Taking the sutta at face value, therefore, we can interpret the term *subharo*, 'easy to support', as referring to how a monk should behave in terms of his economically dependent role with respect to the laity. But there is a deeper and less historically specific principle at work in this part of the sutta. Whether we are monk or lay, or neither one nor the other, we are supported by society at large, and dependent on the labour of innumerable other people for the necessities of life. We do not grow all our own food or draw our own water; we do not build and furnish our own houses or weave and sew all our own clothes.

If we reflect on how it is that we can enjoy so many consumer products for so little outlay – if we think of the hours of cheap labour that go into what we are able to buy for next to nothing – we will find that we are not at all easily supported. There are also environmental and ecological considerations to take into account. The natural and human resources available to our society should not be expended heedlessly or needlessly. The fact that we have the financial resources to help ourselves to what we fancy does not justify our consuming the wealth of the world without consideration for the claims of others – both in the present and in the future – on those same resources. We owe it to the society that supports us to give what we can to support others. There are very few people who would benefit spiritually from being entirely supported by others in the way the traditional monastic sangha was.

The principle behind this term *subharo* therefore comes down to taking from the world and from society no more than you need, and freely contributing whatever you can. You are entitled to rely on others for the help and support that one human being can be reasonably expected to give another, but you also need to be prepared to stand on your own two feet, as far as you can. You cannot expect to be propped up by others as a right.

This principle operates on all levels of exchange, not only on the material and economic level. We need the emotional support of others, for example, but we should not expect from our friends what we are capable of providing for ourselves with a little effort. Once they have helped us back on our feet, we shouldn't expect them to prop us up indefinitely. If you are emotionally needy, you are clearly not yet 'capable', and as such you are not 'easy to support'. You are therefore unlikely to make much progress in meditation. Of course, if you are such a person it is quite possible that you will not understand that you are making undue emotional demands on others, and that their time and energy might be better spent in other ways. In that case it is up to your friends to help you to see the truth of your situation, and perhaps direct you towards getting some therapeutic help, rather than offering 'support' that will just perpetuate the problem.

SIMPLIFYING
Work can be an unhealthy means by which to escape from being alone with oneself and one's feelings.

If you are aiming to be easy to support, the way to do it is to keep your wants and needs to a manageable level, in whatever way you can. This is the ideal to which the term *sallahukavutti* refers: a livelihood, *vutti*, that is *lahuka*, literally 'trifling' or 'light-weight'. It suggests a basic simplicity in one's attitude to life, a determination not to be weighed down by a multiplicity of wants and desires or onerous material commitments. Clearly a taste for hard work, and a relish for the challenge of practical tasks and problems to be overcome, is a virtue, but it is possible to like these things too much for one's own good, especially if they become distractions from more spiritually pressing challenges. So the sutta goes on to say that one should be *appakicco*, 'with little work' or 'with few duties'.

The fact is that one can become too busy even with religious or spiritual activities. Again with reference to the monastic context of early Indian Buddhism, the sutta warns against giving yourself too many things to do. The monk shouldn't be too occupied with performing ceremonies for the laity or running errands for his teachers or preceptors, or even with teaching his own pupils. He should allow himself enough time for study, meditation, reflection, and just spending time quietly by himself – all the things that the lay people in fact support him to do.

Work, in the sense of pleasurable, productive activity, is a necessary part of life for most people. But there is a difference between this and a kind of neurotic, compulsive activity that masquerades as work but is really a way of keeping the deeper emotions at bay. Work can be an unhealthy means by which to escape from being alone with oneself and one's feelings. We should beware of feeling that we have to keep busy, that we can never be without something to do. So yes, by all means work, but don't let busyness be an escape from your true self. Be occupied only with those activities that are really necessary.

MODEST

We should avoid 'getting our feet under the table'
in the course of our involvement with groups,
systems, and ideologies.

The division of labour between monk and lay person has other disadvantages. Relying completely on other people for your support puts you in a passive relationship with regard to them. There is a suggestion of this danger in the sutta, in which the Buddha now enjoins the monk to be *apagabbho kulesu ananugiddho*. Like *subharo*, the term *apagabbho* clearly has to do with the relationship between wandering monks and the lay people upon whom they depend. It is the negative form of *pagabbho*, which means 'impudent', 'over bold', 'tending to push oneself forward', and Saddhatissa translates it quite neatly as 'modesty'. Together with the term that follows, *kulesu ananugiddho*, 'greedy after gifts', it would seem to refer to the danger of monks insinuating themselves into special relationships with particular families. It could happen that a family would end up adopting a particular monk and in a way 'domesticating' him. To avoid this, the sutta directs the monk to avoid making strong connections with anyone or soliciting special favours from them when on his almsround, as this is against the whole spirit of renunciation for which he stands.

Reading between the lines of the sutta, we can see that even the homeless wanderer of the Buddha's day was not necessarily free from attachment to the things that came his way, few as these must have been. He might well be tempted to secure creature comforts and a certain sense of belonging by getting to know certain families, out of a yearning for the approval and acceptance of ordinary people. To guard against this, he is counselled to cultivate a sense of identity based on inner stability and contentment.

But how should we ourselves interpret this exhortation? After all, we don't knock on doors for alms. For us, perhaps, the danger is of depending for our sense of identity upon the acceptance or approbation of others, being afraid of exclusion. The possible result of such dependence is that one is unable to make decisions, hold opinions, dress, eat, or do all manner of other things without reference to the norms of the group whose approval one seeks. To protect ourselves from this, we should avoid making ourselves too much at home in any one human grouping, or identifying with a group too rigidly. We should avoid 'getting our feet under the table' in the course of our involvement with groups, systems, and ideologies. If you are skilled in your good and wish to attain Nirvāṇa, you cannot afford to be too attached to the approval of any group, whether it is your biological family, your cultural or ethnic group, your caste or nationality. A mature individual has an existence, as it were, in his or her own right, without needing to have recourse to the affirmation of any group, be it a family, a community, or even a religious movement. Such a person is capable of finding a sense of fulfilment within the experience of his or her own being, independent of external circumstances.

THE SIXTH SENSE
When you are free from greedy or anxious grasping at objects … you are free to enjoy them fully.

The clarity of purpose discussed thus far finds expression in a particular kind of mindfulness suggested by the term *santindriyo*. This is often translated as 'with senses controlled' or 'with senses disciplined', as though the senses were like wild horses to be reined in and brought under control. But this is not an accurate reflection of the nature of the bodily senses, or an accurate translation of the Pali word. The literal meaning of *santi* is not 'disciplined' but 'calmed', and it is not to the wild horses of the eyes and ears that it refers, but to the wild horse within, the wild horse of the mind.

It is traditional in Buddhism to speak not of five senses but of six: not just the senses of sight, sound, taste, smell, and touch, but also that of the mind. And of all six senses it is the mind that is the origin of craving and attachment. It is only as a mental experience that we need to address the issue of sensory experience at all. The physical senses are in themselves quite pure. Their nature is just to register stimuli. They are being stimulated all the time we are awake, as all kinds of phenomena impinge on them and present themselves to our consciousness. In fact, the physical senses are not so much wild horses as windows or mirrors: they may be obstructed or closed or stained, but they do not determine what degree or quality of light passes through them or is reflected by them. They are themselves incapable of mischief. There is nothing inherently wrong with seeing forms and colours, nothing wrong with hearing sound or tasting food. If our minds were pure, if there were 'in the seen only the seen, in the heard only the heard' (to quote another famous Pali sutta),[9] there would be nothing to pacify, no conflict to resolve.

If, for instance, you were to look at a flower, you might experience an intense perception of colour, scent, perhaps movement, and you might simply appreciate that sensory experience. If you didn't appropriate what you saw or smelled, if you didn't react to it with craving, no unskilful mental state would have arisen from that sense contact. Likewise with a disagreeable or fearful object: if you could respond creatively to the experience, without reacting to it with revulsion or horror, no unskilful mental state would arise. Ideally, this is what we need to be cultivating: the ability to appreciate any sort of sense experience simply for what it is, free from the imposition upon it of our likes and dislikes.

Appreciation is very much part of this activity of mindful awareness. Even though we cannot rely on sense experience for lasting fulfilment, it is nonetheless to be enjoyed on its own level. You need food that is wholesome and nutritious, for example. If it tastes good as well, so much the better. If someone offers you some succulent fruit, for instance, you will appreciate it as both nourishing and delicious. On the other hand, if there is no fruit today, but only porridge, that's perfectly fine too. You remain content, because your good humour is not dependent on having that fruit. This is how the peaceful mind operates in relation to sense experience.

It was once seriously suggested to me that high spiritual attainment made all food taste the same. The person who suggested this – clearly he had quite a high opinion of his own level of attainment – claimed that he no longer tasted rice or potatoes or tea, but simply food and drink in a general sense. This is of course nonsense. When you are free from greedy or anxious grasping at objects, you can become aware of them in all their colour, depth, and vitality as never before. You are free to enjoy them fully. The more aware you become, the more sensitive you are to subtle differences of taste, sound, and so on. This is the middle way between hedonism and hair-shirt asceticism. You don't have to avoid good food, but if your ability to remain happy is too dependent on what you are given to eat, then some degree of renunciation is clearly in order.

To be aware of what is pleasant is fine. It is when we move on to forming a desire for that pleasant experience to stay as it is, and therefore the desire to possess it, that we sow the seed of future dissatisfaction. Likewise, unpleasant sensory experience need not inevitably produce dissatisfaction. It is the mind reacting with ignorance, craving, or revulsion that produces the sense of dissatisfaction. All the objects of the senses – things, people, and experiences – are impermanent, always changing, and when the mind is calm you are able simply to let them be as they are, without the anxious desire to grasp at them or to push them away.

Having said that, we do need to limit the sense experience to which we expose ourselves. The movement from the bare perception of something into the desire to possess it (or move away from it) is taking place all the time, but at such a subtle level that we need a certain degree of mental stillness to be aware of it. By exercising choice over our sensory experience, we aim to calm the mind, withdrawing, in a relative sense, from worldly activity, as a way of simplifying and deepening awareness. There are a thousand and one sensory distractions ready to impinge on our awareness in everyday life, and any one of them can quickly engage our interest in an unguarded moment. Modern forms of publicity and mass communication are expert at seizing the attention and manipulating the emotions so as to induce states of greed, craving, and aversion. They make use of the fact that there are certain ideas, images, sounds, and even smells that will affect most people's minds in a particular way. Popular forms of entertainment, for example, rely on violent or erotic images to hold our attention and keep the mind excited and spellbound. For the average person, at least, it is thus not advisable to give free rein to sensory stimuli. The best time to visit the supermarket or pastry shop is when you are not feeling hungry, and therefore more likely to be drawn into a greedy state of mind by the cleverly arranged displays of tempting titbits on offer.

Our aim, however, is not to shut down perception, blinker the senses, or rigidly control input. Isolating ourselves from experience in this way would produce a brittle, artificial contentment that could not withstand the knocks of ordinary life. When calming the mind's response to the world through the senses, you still act, think, make decisions, and engage with people and with things; but you don't allow your choice of actions to reflect a neurotic and rigid adherence to personal likes and dislikes.

Training the mind may well involve restraining the eye from contact with certain visual objects, and the ear from taking note of certain sounds, but with practice your contentment will not be *dependent* on your living simply. It is fundamentally the mind that has to be pacified, so that it can become more aware of its own movements. Once your mind has become calm, and as your awareness broadens and deepens, you become more sensitive than before to your experience – a sensitiveness that begins to shine through with greater vitality and warmth.

DISCREET

The practical wisdom called for here is ... simply the ability just to keep out of trouble, spiritually speaking.

The ability to find contentment in one's own resources depends on one's having a certain degree of psychological integration in the sense of self-knowledge. You have to get to know the conditions, both internal and external, that tend to produce discontent, and learn how to bring to the fore the inner qualities and resources that support contentment. In other words, you have to be what Saddhatissa translates as 'discreet' and Chalmers as 'quick-witted'. The Pali term *nipako* suggests intelligence in the sense of prudence, the ability to adapt means to ends. It is a practical kind of wisdom. There is also a sense of being able to forestall trouble. The prudent person knows what is likely to result from certain kinds of action within a given situation.

As we have noted, it is the mind that has to be calmed, not the senses. Nonetheless, external conditions are still important. When we make decisions and choices about the kind of environment in which we allow our senses to operate, we therefore need to exercise *nipako*. We owe it to ourselves to look for circumstances that will inspire and support our cultivation of higher states of consciousness. To settle for less when we can do something to change our circumstances is a kind of false contentment that is more like lethargy. Most of these will be circumstances that everybody will find helpful, so it should be a relatively simple matter to find out what they are.

Where discretion becomes particularly necessary is in judging where you as an individual should draw the line in any situation. Rather than falling back on a set of inflexible rules about what you should or should not do, you need to exercise your own judgement, based on what you know about yourself. Whereas one person might find that a certain situation quickly brings about an unskilful mental state, another person might find they can handle the same situation quite skilfully.

In all likelihood a Bodhisattva or an Arhant could encounter crude images and noisy environments and still sustain mental states that were just as skilful as those they would have when looking at beautiful and peaceful scenery. But for the rest of us, the guarding of the senses is a crucial aspect of the practice of mindfulness. Thus one's practice of ethics involves observing for oneself what one's reactions are likely to be. The mark of a morally responsible individual consists in knowing the kind of environment he or she really needs and trying to bring it about.

This is especially true if you are living or working with other people. It is part of your responsibility towards others to take care of yourself, to make sure that you can bring enough contentment into the situation. If you aren't able to be positive, you aren't really pulling your weight, spiritually speaking, and somebody else is going to have to make up for that. Your mental state will impinge on others unless someone else takes up the slack. If you put yourself in a situation in which you are bound to feel discontented, you are being irresponsible with regard to your own welfare, and letting others down as well.

Doing something about this is easier said than done. Somehow you need to cultivate contentment even while you are trying to turn an unsatisfactory situation around. For ordinary human beings, with all their quirks and inconsistencies, their habits, their likes and dislikes, their longing for approval, comfort, sympathy, and all the rest, this is no small thing to ask. In any situation that does not place us under extreme or prolonged pressure, contentment is certainly an achievable goal, but the ability to maintain contentment and inner harmony in absolutely any situation is one of the defining characteristics of a Buddha, Arhant, or Bodhisattva. While it is a goal to aim for, it should not be an expectation placed on a practising Buddhist as a matter of course.

Buddhas and Bodhisattvas, contented as they may be in themselves, will not be 'content' as far as others are concerned. They will see where the situation and circumstances of others can be improved or transformed, and will do something about it. They will recognize how unskilful states of mind and unskilful actions are brought about by certain conditions, and out of compassion will draw attention to that fact and try to remedy the situation.

Such is the contentment and practical wisdom of a Bodhisattva. Of course, this is a far cry from the ordinary human contentment required as one of the preliminary qualities for the development of mettā. This more achievable form of contentment is simply a relative freedom from the inner dissatisfaction that compels us to seek pleasure and fulfilment in external things. Likewise, the practical wisdom called for here is no transcendental quality, but simply the ability just to keep out of trouble, spiritually speaking.

The key characteristic of one who is self-aware is that they are able – indeed find it necessary – to act in accordance with their aspirations and make their own judgements rather than comply with the norms and requirements of any group. If you are an individual, you are able to take responsibility for yourself, for what you do, and for what you think. However, you still need to form relationships with other people. In fact, taking responsibility for your own decisions and experience will make you more truly responsive to the needs of others. Being independent, you are better able to relate to others than if you were to rely on external affirmation and approval for your sense of well-being. That is, you are more able to be ethical.

Morality understood in the Buddhist sense is not so much about rules as about personal growth and progress, both your own and that of those around you. In the spiritual community the group and its norms are ideally replaced by the subtle relationship of kalyāṇa mitratā, spiritual friendship based on that which is wise, skilful, morally beautiful, and true. The spiritual community has as its goal the highest possible development of each of its members, as well as that of the spiritual community itself as a whole. Indeed, it aspires to contribute, at least indirectly, to the ultimate welfare of all beings.

Beyond certain broad categories it is impossible to reduce morality in this sense to a matter of observing rules, of doing some things and not doing other things. Relying on the strict application of rules and regulations seems to work satisfactorily only in the case of simple, straightforward situations. Most circumstances are so complex, and human beings themselves so various, that what is a skilful and beneficial course of action for one person may not help another person – or even that same person at another time. What is right in one set of circumstances might not be right in other circumstances, and what is right for one person might not be right for someone else. This is not to suggest a complete ethical relativism. The point is that, given the complexity of real-life situations, it is difficult to judge exactly how even carefully agreed moral principles will work out in practice, or whether what you are doing is really good for you or for others. Once you begin to sharpen your ethical awareness, situations that had formerly seemed entirely straightforward may begin to raise knotty moral problems.

If you cannot rely on the rules, and, as is often the case, you cannot fall back on a reliable intuitive sense of the skilful thing to do, what is left for you to rely on? The traditional answer is that in this kind of situation it is the opinion of the *viññū* – literally 'those who know' – that is your best guide. In other words, you can place your faith in the informed judgement of those in the spiritual community with more spiritual experience than you. Hence the next verse of the *Karaṇīya Metta Sutta*.

He should not pursue the slightest thing for which other wise men might censure him.

Na ca khuddaṃ samācare kiñci
yena viññū pare upavadeyyuṃ.

THE WISE – WHERE DO WE FIND THEM?

So the person who is skilled in his good and wishes to attain the state of calm, who has the very positive qualities set out in the first two verses of the sutta, should not do even the slightest thing with which those members of the spiritual community who are wise might have cause to find fault. This is a necessary and important criterion for ensuring that your actions are taking you on the right path: to know that those who understand how unethical actions are followed by consequences will not censure you.

But how do you know that they really are wise and that you are not just seeking the approval of the more powerful and influential members of the group? This is a question that is not always easy to answer. In extreme cases it may be easy to see the difference between conformity to group values and reliance upon the advice of the spiritual community. But obviously there will be intermediate cases where you might not be so sure. Situations may arise in which you are uncertain whether you are acting on the advice of 'the wise' because you want to be accepted by the group and fear rejection, or because you respect the greater spiritual maturity of those you are consulting. Either way, their opinion will matter to you. But a reliance on the opinion of 'the wise', in the sense that the term has in this sutta, is really a question of how far you regard your spiritual friends as being a truly spiritual community, rather than just another social group.

The wise have to be those in whom you have real confidence, those whom you know have your best interests at heart. But such trust can come only from experience, in other words from giving them some provisional trust. You may have taken their advice on trust in the past and found from experience that in some circumstances their judgement is more reliable than your own. You may also know and trust other people who have found them trustworthy. However you garner this testimony of experience, it takes time to discover whether or not the members of what you have identified – again provisionally – as the spiritual community have a degree of vision, skill, and maturity that you yourself do not yet possess.

If we are going to be sceptical about those who appear to be 'the wise', we have also to be sceptical about our own objectivity. Perhaps it should not come as too much of a surprise to discover that we are inclined to doubt the judgement of the wise. They have, by definition, a different perspective from our own. The fact that they really do know, and we do not, means that we cannot see things quite as they see them, because we lack their vision and their level of understanding.

In order to be receptive to the advice or censure of the wise, you therefore have to have a personal relationship with them. Only by knowing your spiritual friends well can you be sure that they know you well also, and have your best interests at heart, indeed may understand your interests better than you do yourself. You can then accept their judgement even when it does not correspond with your own. A spiritual friend is someone who knows you well and cares about you. They won't see your welfare in quite the same way as you do; they will see beyond what you want for yourself – almost as a parent sees that the welfare of their child does not necessarily lie in what the child wants. But the spiritual friend will be at the same time disinterested. They won't be upset if you don't do what they suggest; they don't have an emotional axe to grind.

SPIRITUAL FRIENDS: OUR MORAL TOUCHSTONE

With mettā you can always see through that greed or stupidity to the beauty of the human being: it is through mettā that you can hold the two together, the ugly truth and the beautiful reality.

In the spiritual community, the rigid application of rules is replaced by something far more subtle: a living network of friendship and communication centred on the highest shared ideals. Essentially, friendship within the spiritual community is based on mettā, on an appreciation of the other person's virtues and faults alike. Feeling mettā does not blind you to the facts. If someone is greedy or stupid, you see that they are. But with mettā you can always see through that greed or stupidity to the beauty of the human being: it is through mettā that you can hold the two together, the ugly truth and the beautiful reality. Indeed, if you don't see the one, you won't really see the other, not clearly anyway.

So feeling mettā does not mean seeing the inner beauty of people while deliberately blinding yourself to their weaknesses and imperfections. Nor is it about *appreciating* their weaknesses, or even appreciating them in spite of their weaknesses. It is more subtle than that: it is more like an aesthetic appreciation, or the clear-sighted love of a parent for their child. You see the child's faults and weaknesses, and the qualities he or she needs to develop, but your knowledge of these frailties has no effect on your love. Indeed, it is in the nature of real love to nurture the loved person without cherishing any illusions about them.

The wise have an ethical sensibility that is the product of their own experience and transcends the legalistic application of rules. They don't look at your actions in isolation, but in the context of your emerging individuality. It is like the aesthetic sensibility of someone who really understands painting or literature. They know quite intuitively what painting or literature is. Someone who knows what writing is can start reading something and know after a few paragraphs whether it is worth continuing or not. A person, too, is all of a piece. (Of course, the difference between a book and a person is that it is always worth continuing with a person.)

Also, when our spiritual friends become aware of certain of our actions, they may not know all the circumstances, but they will have an accurate sense of whether those actions are skilful or not. For our own part, as the sutta says, we would do well to give the spiritually mature the respect they deserve, and heed their opinion. That opinion will not necessarily come in the form of censure. It is generally more subtle than that. You may detect some change in them, or they may detect some change in you. Either way, you begin to be conscious of some disharmony between you – not in a dramatic, obvious way, but more a sense that you are no longer on the same wavelength, no longer really communicating.

It may well be that your spiritual friends are oblivious to any change in the relationship with you. They may have said nothing to you. Nonetheless, you may start to get the uncomfortable feeling that they are displeased with you, even angry or reproachful, and you may begin to feel resentment and even anger towards them, even though they have no idea what is going on. Surprisingly, perhaps, this sort of misapprehension is one of the more useful products of spiritual friendship, for it shows that your ethical sense, your sense of shame, is developing. You know in your heart that you have started to go astray, to slide a bit, and this is your way of allowing your guilty conscience to make its presence felt. In time, if they are at all mindful of their relationship with you, your spiritual friends will begin to notice that something is amiss, that you seem rather uneasy, perhaps a little sullen or unforthcoming. When they probe gently and kindly for an explanation of your changed demeanour, you may start wondering how this has happened, and how you can reestablish communication and harmony and put your friendship back on track. Once they are able to say that they are not angry with you and that you have done nothing to displease them, you can take the opportunity to say that well, actually, you do have something on your conscience, if only they knew.

Clearing the air with your friends in this way, you come back into harmony with the spiritual community, all through your openness to the possibility that your spiritual friends, those who really know you, might disapprove of what you're doing, even, as the sutta says, on account of 'the slightest thing'. The essential element is your own sensitivity to the ethical sensibility of others, not your fear of punishment or disfavour. If you feel that your spiritual friends are beginning to disapprove of you, that they are not quite at ease with the way you are, the chances are that you should take special care. It is not your spiritual friends who have changed and started to drift out of contact. It is you.

Outside the spiritual community, people are not as a rule committed to this expansive aspiration to grow and to see others grow. Without spiritual friendship and mettā, what masquerades as helpful criticism may be no more than a thinly veiled form of one-upmanship. If the effect of your 'helpful' criticism is to leave someone feeling downcast, it is not an expression of mettā. Outside the spiritual community (and sometimes, despite our best efforts, within it) the emotional basis for interpersonal communication is so fraught with competitiveness, not to say aggression, that even a well-intended criticism can hurt and be wide of the mark.

In the context of a genuine spiritual friendship, however, I would go so far as to say that if you were to point out to someone that they had acted unskilfully, even if this were painful for them to hear, they would feel better for your having told them. Perhaps these difficult situations, in which openness and honesty are likely to involve a certain amount of pain, are the real test of mettā and of the depth of our friendship. If your straight talking expresses a sense of moral superiority – however justified – and a wish to put someone down or make them feel small, you are clearly not motivated by mettā. But as long as your communication is infused by a genuine feeling of mettā, your friend will feel not crushed but liberated by what you have said, and the friendship will become stronger as a result.

How you stand in relation to your spiritual friends is a very good touchstone of where you stand ethically. Whether or not your friends are happy with how you are progressing tells you whether or not you need to be concerned about your spiritual practice. However, it must be emphasized that the censure of the wise is not an authority to be followed blindly. Whatever you do must be your own clear choice, for which you take full responsibility. Group censure is essentially a demand on the part of the group elders that you conform to the standards and norms of the group. By contrast, in the spiritual community, the criticism that you receive comes ideally from a different kind of attitude – though, of course, even within the spiritual community censure and advice is sometimes offered and received in the spirit of the group.

Chapter Three

CULTIVATING METTĀ

May all beings be happy and secure, may their hearts be wholesome!

Sukhino vā khemino hontu
sabbe sattā bhavantu sukhitattā

We have now come to a natural break in the sutta. Up to this point, the teaching has been about setting up preparatory conditions for the effective cultivation of mettā. One might even say that if you fulfil these conditions – if you are capable, straight, upright, and so on – you will be in such a skilful, healthy frame of mind that you can't help wishing others well. It will be the natural thing for you to do, not only when you sit down to meditate but all the time. Your mental and emotional state will be so positive that, quite spontaneously, you will wish for others to enjoy health, happiness, security, and peace of mind.

The next section of the sutta begins with a phrase that sums up the generosity, the sincere and heartfelt regard for others, in which the cultivation of mettā consists. We wish simply that beings may be happy and secure and that their hearts may be wholesome. *Khemino* means secure, that is, free from danger, free from disturbance, free from fear. *Sukhi* simply means happy. *Sukhitattā* is translated here as 'their hearts be wholesome', but the suffix *atta* means 'self' or 'being', so the Pali term literally means 'of happy self' or 'happy-hearted'. To be precise, the whole phrase could be translated as 'May they be those whose self is happiness.' This makes it clear that you want their happiness, their bliss, to be entirely within themselves, not dependent on external circumstances. In their essence they should be happy. Happiness is not something they should *have*, but something that they should *be*. It is happiness in this sense, together with the mettā that produces such happiness for oneself and wants it for others, that characterizes the spiritual community. If you don't find a greater degree of mettā and happiness in the spiritual community than you find in the world generally, it isn't really a spiritual community.

The broad message of the first section of the sutta is that if we want to enjoy positive mental states, we must pay attention to our everyday activities – our thoughts and volitions, our speech and actions, throughout the day. We should raise our consciousness in the only way that can generate a genuine transformation of being, by living out our ideals, by turning skilful actions into skilful habits, to the point where our mind naturally tends towards states of clarity, concentration, and happiness.

This opening section of the sutta has essentially been a preparation for what is to come. The wish expressed in this verse, that all beings may be happy and secure, is more than a vague hope. It introduces the section of the sutta that is concerned with the technique of meditating on loving-kindness, and thus designed to help us develop that aspiration for the well-being of others in a very real way. It is in the practice of formal meditation, when the mind is brought to bear directly on the mind, that mettā is cultivated most intensely.

The next section, again of two-and-a-half verses, sets forth the means by which we can develop that mettā. It does so through what is effectively a description of the mettā bhāvanā practice, the meditation on loving-kindness taught by the Buddha himself, which is, as we have seen, an indispensable aspect of the path to the attainment of the state of calm, or Nirvāṇa.

Whatever living beings there be: feeble or strong, tall, stout or medium, short, small or large, without exception; seen or unseen, those dwelling far or near, those who are born or those who are to be born, may all beings be happy!

Ye keci pāṇabhūt' atthi
tasā va thāvarā vā anavasesā
dīghā vā ye mahantā vā
majjhimā rassakā aṇukathūlā

Diṭṭhā vā ye vā adiṭṭhā
ye ca dūre vasanti avidūre
bhūtā vā sambhavesī vā;
sabbe sattā bhavantu sukhitattā.

THE WHOLE WORLD OF BEINGS

The aim of any meditation practice is to train the mind and thereby to heighten and transform consciousness. In the mettā bhāvanā meditation this training takes the form of various explicitly formulated aspirations and wishes for the welfare of different classes of beings, and for their abstaining from various forms of unskilful behaviour. Calling to mind those categories of beings and directing thoughts of loving-kindness towards them, you engender loving-kindness towards real people, as many of them as possible. In the course of your meditation you bring to mind all the weak, helpless beings, all the strong and healthy ones, and then beings of various shapes and sizes, right down to those beings who are too small to be seen at all – which presumably refers to microbes and single-celled organisms, as well as to those beyond human perception in other ways. You call to mind those who are as far away as you can possibly imagine, and those nearby. So this is one systematic way of developing mettā. In other forms of the practice you concentrate on the geographical differentiation of beings by directing your mettā towards all beings in the eastern quarter, all those in the south, the west, and the north, and finally all those above you and below you. You then call to mind those born and those unborn, thus reminding yourself that your mettā is not limited by time or by space.

In this way the sutta addresses the central problems of cultivating mettā. Firstly, there is the sheer scale of its reference. If
you sat down to meditate and found yourself immediately full of
mettā, you could no doubt direct that mettā towards any class of
beings that you wished. But probably very few people would
find themselves in that position. A methodical approach is
therefore necessary if you are going to get anywhere with the
practice. Otherwise, you would wish for all beings without
number to be well and, after a brief but mind-boggling attempt
to visualize them all, you would pass on to the next meditation.

The second problem is that mettā is impersonal in the sense
that it has no specific object, while at the same time it is not at all
'woolly'. A vague sense that you wish everyone well together
with a generalized impression of 'everyone' won't do. Ultimately mettā may be without an object, but to begin with you
have to develop it in relation to actual specific persons, otherwise your emotions will not get involved. You have to begin
closer to home. The same goes for other reflective practices: the
contemplation of impermanence, for example.

Another practical reason for the sutta's detailed roster of the
recipients of mettā is to counteract any irrational dislike you
may have for certain categories of people. One would do well to
draw up a list of one's own prejudices to make the list as inclusive as possible. You might have a prejudice against tall people
or fat people, or men with beards, or blonde women. Since there
is no accounting for taste, or indeed distaste, it is as well to
include these formally in the practice, as well as trying to
become aware of those categories of beings you have overlooked
altogether.

THE METTĀ BHĀVANĀ PRACTICE

The technique of the mettā bhāvanā is based on the principle that the more strongly you feel mettā towards one person, the easier it will be to experience the same emotion towards someone else.

There are many variations of the mettā bhāvanā practice, including the one outlined by the Buddha here and a version contained in the *Visuddhimagga*, Buddhaghosa's fifth century exposition of the Buddha's teaching as found in the Pali canon. But all the variations share their working method with other Buddhist contemplations and meditations for the cultivation of particular kinds of awareness or understanding. In the contemplation of impermanence, for example, you call to mind a number of things that can be identified as impermanent, some quite easily, others with a little more difficulty. This helps you to deepen a fundamental awareness of impermanence as being in the nature of all conditioned existence. The general methodology is the same in the case of the cultivation of mettā. Universal loving-kindness is not the easiest of emotions to cultivate, but there do exist various effective stage-by-stage ways of doing it.

The more or less standard way of practising the mettā bhāvanā is in five stages, each of which takes your mettā deeper. First you generate mettā towards yourself, then towards a good friend, thirdly towards a 'neutral' person – someone whom you know but for whom you have no particularly strong feelings – and fourthly towards an 'enemy' – someone you find difficult for some reason. In the fifth stage you try to feel mettā for all four persons equally, then conclude the practice by radiating your mettā outward in wider and wider circles. The main thing is to get your mettā flowing; and bringing to mind the four different persons and then 'equalizing' the mettā seems to do that most effectively.

Thereafter, you can either go all round the world in your imagination, country by country, continent by continent, or you can take up the traditional method of dividing the globe into the four directions or quarters – north, south, east, and west – and radiating your mettā in each direction in turn. Another method is to consider variations on the sutta's different categories of beings – say the rich, the poor, the well, the sick, the young, the old, animals, birds, fish, and so on. You can try any combination of these approaches to the fifth and last stage. Once you have got the mettā flowing it doesn't really matter which method you follow, as long as you include everyone, indeed all beings, everywhere. The technique of the mettā bhāvanā is based on the principle that the more strongly you feel mettā towards one person, the easier it will be to experience the same emotion towards someone else who is less obviously a candidate for your affection. By bringing all those categories of beings to mind, one after the other, you give yourself the best possible opportunity to amplify and deepen your experience of mettā.

Let none deceive another, nor despise any person whatsoever in any place. Let him not wish any harm to another in anger or ill will.

Na paro paraṃ nikubbetha
nâtimaññetha katthacinaṃ kañci
vyārosanā paṭighasaññā
nâññamaññassa dukkham iccheyya.

RESPONDING WITH METTĀ

Having established the scope of the practice, the sutta moves on to explore further the quality of mettā we are aiming to develop. Although the form of the practice in five stages is not explicitly mentioned here, each stage presents its own challenges when it comes to keeping the flow of mettā going. But before we look at these in turn, we can get from the text a general sense of what we are aiming to do. This verse shows us the response of mettā to the betrayals and slights, the abuse and malice, that come to us from other people, and also, by implication, the positive spirit in which we should acknowledge our own unskilful actions. To begin with, if you truly desire the happiness of others as much as you desire your own, there will be no question of misleading them or lying to them. Any attempt at deception is almost always motivated by calculated self-interest, which is the very antithesis of mettā. Even when no calculation is involved, it is dreadfully easy to belittle or humiliate someone with a few casual words. But although it is so easily done, it is no small matter: it betrays a terrible failure of mettā, a thoughtless discounting of another person.

This translation unusually renders *dukkha* as 'harm'. The term generally refers to misery, unhappiness, or even simple disappointment, none of which unpleasant or painful states of mind is necessarily connected to physical harm. *Dukkha* can also be understood to mean the opposite of peace or *santa*, the ultimate goal or good which is our real aim in life and towards which the Buddha, the Śāntināyaka, directs us through his teaching. *Dukkha* is the fundamental experience of unease inherent in conditioned existence. In this context, however, *dukkha* refers specifically to suffering wished upon us by someone else, out of anger or ill will. As such, it can indeed be translated as 'harm'.

To be angry is not necessarily to wish harm upon someone. The Pali term translated here as 'anger', *osanā*, is the momentary flash of rage that might cause you to lose your temper. It is the result of frustrated energy: you want to do something, have something, or see something happen, and when your wish is blocked in some way, the energy that has been restricted or frustrated bursts through in an explosion of bad temper. Anger is an emotion of the moment. If there is a desire to cause harm, it is momentary and instinctive.

Paṭigha, on the other hand, translated here as 'ill will', is more sinister, involving a conscious, even calculated, desire to do harm. *Paṭigha* is thus a much stronger term than simple ill will. At the very least it means 'violent malice', and it usually refers to a state of rage: an uncontrolled, unreasoned, almost mindless determination to wreak harm and suffering on another person. *Paṭigha* can be taken to stand for all those deeply unskilful states that are antithetical to mettā. As well as malice there is cruelty, a gratuitous pleasure in inflicting harm, which in its extreme form becomes sadism. The key difference between these deeply un-pleasant mental states and anger is that whereas malice, cruelty, and sadism continue over time, indeed are sometimes nursed for years, anger is an emotion of the moment. But if anger remains unexpressed, it will turn into something that settles down and anchors itself, to become resentment or even hatred. It is hatred, not anger, that is the real enemy of mettā. It is the conscious, fixed, and settled desire to do harm which we have to guard against, and which is hatred's defining quality.

Negative emotions are more closely connected than we might think; they are all expressions of the fundamental wish to do harm to others. Hatred can arise in many forms, in many kinds of situation. It is when some everyday occurrence sparks off a momentary sense of ill will that the deeper, darker residue of hatred emerges. When we get angry, our sudden anger can toss a match into a kind of tinder-box of hatred, sparking off cruelty, rage, or malice. If we are prone to anger in the sense of *osanā*, it can be difficult to rein it in, because once we have lost our tem-per we are no longer susceptible to reason. We need to be espe-cially on our guard when we feel our anger is justified, as a sense of righteous indignation opens the gates for more destructive emotions. All the same, compared to *paṭigha*, anger is a relatively healthy reaction. Sometimes letting off a bit of steam in an innocuous context is better than bottling it up.

WHY DO WE HATE?
There is such a thing as hatred at first sight.

Hatred is the antithesis of human growth and development. With craving and ignorance, it is one of the three 'unskilful roots' (*akusala mūlas*) that feed and sustain our lower nature. It is perhaps strange to reflect that hatred is a uniquely human quality. Animals may compete to the death for natural resources, fighting one another, feeding upon one another, even killing for amusement, and yet, as far as we know, they do not harbour any conscious intention to do harm. So why do humans have this particular capacity for evil?

Although we share a common ancestry, human beings have a quality that animals do not: the capacity for reason. It can lead to great good, of course, but unfortunately it can also lead to hatred. We experience suffering as animals do, but we also have an ability to seek and find causes for our unhappiness, and to extrapolate from knowledge of our own motives in such a way as to attribute motives to other beings. According to the seventeenth-century Dutch philosopher Spinoza, if you have a feeling of pain accompanied by the idea of the pain's external cause, your response will be hatred towards that external cause.[10] Hatred, in other words, is as much an idea as a feeling. We hate whatever or whomever we see as responsible for the unhappiness we feel.

But this still does not really explain what happens. Indeed, there seems to be no rational explanation. After all, if you were suffering and realized that another person was the cause, and if you were able to keep out of their way or to stop them from hurting you, there would be no reason for your wanting to inflict harm upon them. Unfortunately, however, when you are suffering you don't just want to remove the instrument of your unhappiness; you also have an urge to retaliate by inflicting a degree of suffering on them that will satisfy you emotionally – an urge that has no basis in reason.

Another thing that marks us out from animals is our consciousness of the passing of time, and this also plays a part in the arising of hatred. Every time we allow the memory of a supposed wrong to run through our mind, hatred accumulates until a fixed attitude develops. From then on, whatever our enemy does we interpret their actions according to that fixed view, and they simply cannot do anything to please us.

While emotions are essentially active, we nonetheless create them from the raw material of feelings, and these come to us passively, to be taken up and given meaning and direction by the activity of the mind. Feelings in themselves, whether pleasant or unpleasant, are karmically neutral; they are the results of our previous actions. As such, it is how we deal with them, not the fact of our feeling them, that is of decisive importance. If you have a painful experience, you need not manufacture hatred out of it. If you do, you render yourself liable to further painful feeling in the future because by reacting with anger you have created fresh – and unskilful – karma. So hatred is not something that just happens to you. Like any other emotion – craving, say, or mettā – it is something you do. Feelings are presented to you, you experience them; but whether you create harmful or helpful emotions out of them is up to you.

The point is that our dislikes and resentments are often not based on anything people have actually done. They may come from our irrational expectations, or they may be a matter of interpersonal chemistry. There is such a thing as hatred at first sight. Someone may have an emotional quality that you pick up and react against without your even knowing them, or they may unconsciously remind you of someone else, perhaps a parent or sibling, an ex-lover, or someone else from your past with whom you have had difficulties. This is what psychologists call projection. Likewise, a small incident can spark off an outburst of anger or irritability, awakening an emotion connected with some suppressed incident or series of incidents long ago and far away.

A great deal of our latent tendency towards ill will is likely to stem from our early conditioning. It is easy to recognize people whose early life has been comparatively untroubled, as they are relatively straightforward, open, and receptive. Others are much more suspicious, reserved, and wary, and this may be a result of their early experience. It seems that many of us have a certain residual resentment, or even hatred, that lingers from our childhood and tends to attach itself to objects and people as we make our way through adult life.

Sometimes these negative feelings are found to be attached to close relatives, if we are prepared to look for them there, although many people are shocked at the idea of feeling animosity towards their nearest and dearest. When such feelings do come out into the open, the resulting family disturbance can be particularly painful. If you think there is no one you dislike, it might be revealing to try putting one of your relatives in the fourth stage of the mettā bhāvanā, in which mettā is directed towards an 'enemy', and see what happens. If we live with someone, or work closely with them, or share a circle of friends with them, and have no particular reason to dislike them, we often fail to realize that, all the same, we *do* dislike them. It seems to be a sort of rule that there will always be someone we dislike among our acquaintances or colleagues. When that person leaves, another person with whom we have previously been on good terms may well take their place, to be the next object for the residue of hatred that is so difficult to shift from the human psyche. This is why removing someone from a situation of conflict rarely solves the problem in the long run.

We should try not to feel discouraged by all this. It is true that to wake up in the morning with an overwhelming wish for the happiness and bliss of absolutely everyone is highly unusual even if one aspires to do so. Even after a great deal of intense effort in meditation, a tidal wave of universal love is unlikely to sweep us off our feet and carry us away. We shouldn't really be surprised. In trying to cultivate mettā we are swimming against the current of our human nature as it has evolved over millions of years from its animal origins. Sometimes we simply feel like a rest. As we struggle against the stream of our habitual negativity, mettā seems just too much to ask of ourselves. The tendency to feel hatred for others, even for people who pose no threat, comes all too easily to us. It is a basic human trait. It should be no surprise that the world is so full of conflicts, wars, and fatal misunderstandings. As beings with reflexive consciousness, with a sense of ourselves as continuous identities moving through time, our defences are naturally directed against the threat of attack, not just upon our bodies but also upon our fragile sense of who we think we are. This is why cultivating mettā is such a challenge. It is an attempt to reverse our usual way of experiencing the world and ourselves.

If hatred is a specifically human reaction to a threat, in its most primitive form it originates from any threat to our specifically human sense of self, the most basic sense of who we are. Indeed, to identify with a 'self' in that limited sense is to open ourselves up to that primal threat. Thus to identify with a self is to be susceptible to the arising of hatred. If we think in terms of karma and rebirth, we have been prone to hatred for as long as we have been embodied human beings. It is as though hatred was woven into the very fabric of our being. Since our first human birth we have reacted with hatred to all those situations that threatened the integrity of our continued existence. When a human being experiences this sense of being threatened, there is more at stake than territory or physical safety. We are afraid for our personal identity, our very sense of self, the sense of 'I' that enables a human being to interact and form relationships in much more complex ways than animals can. A threat to the self is a threat not just to our physical well-being but to our psychological security.

If you succeeded in perfecting the practice of the mettā bhāvanā, it would suggest that you no longer felt any threat from anybody and therefore that you no longer identified your being with your contingent personality. But for as long as you are a worldly personality, the potential for hatred will always be there. You can detect it in yourself sometimes – a little flash of undiluted hatred, often when you least expect it.

THE ENEMY WITHIN
How strange it is that we do not quite naturally and wholeheartedly wish others the deepest happiness and bliss!

It is painful to realize that a mind dogged by hatred or irritability continues to harbour a stock of resentment regardless of circumstances, a residue of ill will that will always seek out an object in order to express itself. But such apparently irrational reactions are not necessarily a bad thing. If we never catch sight of our projections, how will we learn to see through them? Psychological projection is unconscious, but by bringing our unconscious reactions into awareness, we can begin to act more appropriately and put down the psychological burdens we have been carrying.

To transform emotions we need to feel them, but in doing so we have to take into account an external reality with which our feelings and urges are not necessarily in touch. We should take care to do this especially if, as is likely, that external reality involves other people. No one can dispute that we feel what we feel. But we need to ask ourselves whether our feelings correspond to reality, whether they are adequate to the situation. From the authoritative way in which many people speak about how they feel, it would seem that they believe that invoking their feelings excuses them from considering objective reality, and that their feelings about it constitute a fully adequate assessment of the situation. Of course, no one should be allowed to get away with this. By all means have emotions – be as emotional as you like – but let them be true to the situation. Don't dress up peevishness or fury as clear thinking and straight talking. If the intellect is to support the emotions, the emotions have to return the favour and support the intellect.

When we are indulging in a subjective and perhaps negative emotion, we very often know in our heart of hearts that our response is not really true to the way things are. When we get angry with someone for a trivial reason, we know – if we are even just a little aware – that the situation does not justify that emotional reaction. When this happens, instead of thinking, 'Oh, I must get rid of my negative emotions,' ask yourself, 'What is the objective situation? Are my emotions appropriate to what is really going on?'

The harmful states that are the enemies of mettā can arise in many different forms, gross and subtle. If you are in a happy, up-beat mood and you mix with people who are not, they may want to share your happiness, but it is also possible that they will prefer to see you as being no less unhappy than they are themselves. They may resent your happiness and feel they have to resist it, even destroy it, as if it were an affront or a challenge to them. Perhaps they want you to show their misery a little respect, or suspect that you are feeling superior and smug. Humans are contradictory beings. How strange it is that we do not quite naturally and wholeheartedly wish others the deepest happiness and bliss! It's as if we feel that there is only so much happiness to go round and that if others are happy there is less happiness left over for us. Certainly people often feel they have a limited quantity of love, to be preserved for close friends and family. But of course the happiness of others cannot do us or them anything but good. Our task in practising the mettā bhāvanā is to learn to extend our mettā beyond this small circle, bit by bit, until it encompasses all beings. In the five-stage version of the practice we begin very close to home indeed: with ourselves. This makes perfect sense. If, as we have seen, the enemy is within, it is within that the enemy needs to be tackled – indeed, needs to be transformed from an enemy into a friend.

DOING THE METTĀ BHĀVANĀ
FIRST STAGE: METTĀ FOR ONESELF

There is a place for selflessness in Buddhism, but not for acquiescence in the face of ill-treatment or a grey and unrewarding environment. Human beings need food, light, space, periods of peace and quiet, human companionship, friendship, and so on. We are naturally geared to look for delight in the world.

You simply cannot develop much loving-kindness towards anyone else if you are on bad terms with yourself, or if you are uncomfortable with what you find out about yourself when all your external supports and comforts are removed. This is why in the first stage of the mettā bhāvanā meditation you begin by cultivating mettā towards yourself. Most people find that this is not at all easy. Only too often the residue of hatred within us is directed towards ourselves.

The solution for many of us lies in our relationships with other people. One way to learn to feel mettā towards yourself is through becoming aware that someone else feels good will towards you, and in this way coming to feel it for yourself. This is rather tricky. When you don't have mettā for yourself, you experience an emptiness, a hunger, and you look for love from someone else to fill that void and make you feel better, at least for the time being. You clutch at love, demanding it as compensation for the unconditional acceptance that you are unable to give yourself. But this can only be a substitute for the real thing. You try to squeeze as much love as you can get out of others, even though that love is something only you can give yourself. It is as though you need them to do it for you. Being dependent on their love, you cannot care for their welfare except in relation to yourself; you cannot feel mettā for them because of your own neediness. For many people this is surely a depressingly familiar picture.

But if you find yourself in this situation, all is not lost. By calmly reasoning with yourself, you can begin to turn that misapprehension around, using the 'substitute' love shown by others to help you develop mettā towards yourself. If they can feel good will towards you, you can learn to feel the same positive emotion towards yourself, and thus gradually learn to stand on your own feet emotionally. Even though you may have begun with the assumption that you were not worth much, you learn from the other person that you were mistaken and thus begin to appreciate your own worth. You allow the knowledge that another person feels that you are genuinely worthwhile to percolate through your mind. You can learn to love yourself, in other words, by realizing that someone else really values you.

Feeling mettā for oneself is often simply a question of dropping the habit of self-criticism and allowing the objective reality of the situation to arise. Whatever you have done, however great your failings, the honest intention to develop mettā towards yourself and all living beings can be a source of happiness in itself. Feeling mettā for oneself is the keystone of contentment – and when you are contented, you can maintain your equanimity no matter in what circumstances you find yourself. It is a resilient, deeply-rooted state of peace, a source of energy and confidence. Contentment is, moreover, an inherently active state, with nothing of the resignation or passivity that is sometimes associated with it. The contented person is both inspired and an inspiration to others. It isn't a question of just gritting your teeth and grinding your way through some awful situation. There is a place for selflessness in Buddhism, but not for acquiescence in the face of ill-treatment or a grey and unrewarding environment. Human beings need food, light, space, periods of peace and quiet, human companionship, friendship, and so on. We are naturally geared to look for delight in the world. But if you are contented, you can find delight in the world around you, even when you don't have everything you would like.

The way to cultivate contentment is to bring a lighter touch to your experience. It is to enjoy what is enjoyable in it, but not to become attached to your pleasures, nor overwhelmed when things appear not to be going your way, in the knowledge that both the pleasures and the pains of life are impermanent. Contentment comes from being aware that as long as you depend on external objects for a sense of well-being, your happiness can never be guaranteed.

Developing mettā consists largely of finding contentment in oneself and living by that. Once it becomes a way of life, one stands a good chance of communicating that peace of mind to everyone with whom one comes into contact. Thus, the first stage of the mettā bhāvanā practice flows naturally into the second.

DOING THE METTĀ BHĀVANĀ
SECOND STAGE: METTĀ FOR A FRIEND
A trusting and open friendship is an excellent context within which to bring our fears and antagonisms to the surface and begin to lay them aside.

In the second stage of the practice we call to mind a good friend and direct our mettā towards them. But if our ultimate aim is to feel mettā for everyone, doesn't this carry with it the danger that we will get this far and no further? Isn't it rather exclusive? Here we need to take a pragmatic approach. Although we can do our best to respond positively to everyone, if we are going to explore friendship in any great depth we can do this in practice with only a limited number of people. Friendship requires a level of trust and intimacy that can arise only through spending a lot of time with a person, becoming a significant part of their life and allowing them to become a significant part of our own. We need not think of our circle of friends as being exclusive; it is simply a fact that we cannot develop depth and intensity in our relationships without making a firm decision to deepen our friendships with just a few people. This remains true even when one has a great deal of spiritual experience. Perhaps after years of practice you will no longer experience partiality in your friendships, and will be able to be equally friendly towards anyone you happen to meet, taking life as it comes and relating to everyone equally warmly and with an equally genuine desire for their well-being. But with the best will in the world, your capacity for friendship will still be limited by the number of people with whom you are realistically able to come into contact.

Thus one can cultivate mettā as a universal and ever-expanding care for all beings, whether near or far, while at the same time enjoying substantial relationships of trust and affection with those with whom one has chosen to enter into a closer relationship. Committed friendship demands personal contact, and that requires both time and opportunity. But a friendly disposition is another matter. There is no limit to the number of people towards whom we can feel genuinely friendly, and with whom we could potentially be friends. And that friendliness, however strongly felt, can only improve the depth of our existing friendships.

Committed friendship obviously involves openness, and this calls for patience and empathy when what our friends reveal to us turns out to be difficult or even hurtful. A trusting and open friendship is an excellent context within which to bring our fears and antagonisms to the surface and begin to lay them aside. But if this is to happen, the friendship must have a spiritual dimension, because hatred is far more than the psychological phenomenon that we have been examining so far. Just as mettā is a spiritual rather than a psychological quality, so its antithesis, hatred, is not just a psychological state, but a spiritually destructive force operating within us.

It is perhaps not surprising that when we start to practise the later stages of the mettā bhāvanā we can find the going difficult. We may even discover, if we are honest with ourselves, that despite our good intentions we do not as a rule experience much desire for the happiness and well-being of even our closest friends. A famous moralist once observed that 'in the misfortune of our best friends, we always find something which is not displeasing to us'.[11] It would seem that even our friends represent some kind of threat. Perhaps this is why ex-lovers are able to do each other so much harm, and why the break-up of a marriage can be so acrimonious: both partners know each other's weak

spots only too well. It is the person with whom you have fully
lowered your guard who can do you the most damage if the relationship changes. It is all about power. If some misfortune be-
falls our friends and they are brought down a peg or two, or
suffer some disappointment, they are made, as it were, less
powerful in relation to us, and the threat is to some extent removed. Sometimes we cannot help finding pleasure in that,
however fond of them we might be. If you are very observant
and honest with yourself, you will notice these little flashes of
pleasure from time to time at the adversity suffered by even
your dearest friends. It is sad but true.

At the same time – and this is an encouraging thought – we
don't have to act on our feelings. Our task is to experience our
negative emotions and then find a way to change them. If we
never get to know these emotions, if we indulge them unthinkingly or try to deny them, no transformation will be possible.
One of the skills you need to develop as a meditator is therefore
to learn to broaden the scope of your emotional awareness,
without allowing completely unmindful expression of what you
start to feel. This is by no means easy: it requires experience, patience, the clarity and kindness of your friends, and gentle per-
sistence in the mettā bhāvanā practice.

DOING THE METTĀ BHĀVANĀ
THIRD STAGE: FEELING METTĀ FOR
A NEUTRAL PERSON

*Just as the sun is not selective in the giving of its light
and warmth, when you feel mettā, you don't choose its
recipients or keep it for those you deem worthy of it.*

In the third stage of the mettā bhāvanā, you direct mettā towards someone you know hardly at all, someone who has only a

very minor walk-on part in your life – perhaps the man who sells you your newspaper in the morning, or the woman you pass in the park when you're walking your dog. To see the point of this stage, we need to examine our emotional life a little further. Although we may not like to think so, in the usual run of things our experience of what we imagine to be positive emotion is likely to be sketchy and intermittent. Whether or not we are aware of it, this is partly because we tend to limit our affection to those we deem deserving of it, usually those who are likely to re-turn the favour. But the chief characteristic of mettā is that it is entirely without self-interest. It is not possessive or selfish, and has nothing to do with appetite. This is why 'friendliness', although it may seem insipid, translates mettā more accurately than 'love'. Being applied only to other sentient beings, and hav-ing an inherently outgoing quality, friendliness is more likely to be relatively free of self-interest.

I say 'relatively' because a great deal of what we think of as friendliness and even friendship involves a need for something in return. When we give affection we want something back, and when a little intensity develops in our friendships we can end up with a dependency that has something of the nature of an unspoken contract. The Pali term for this mixture of honest affection and an expectation of some return is *pema* (the Sanskrit is *prema*). It is usually translated as 'affection' in the limited sense of ordinary human fellowship, and it is contrasted with mettā, which is the corresponding, more spiritual emotion.

Pema is often understood to be the natural affection and good will that arises within the family group, and it is undoubtedly a positive emotion. Indeed, it is the cement that holds social life to-gether. Expressing warmth and affection to your family mem-bers and close friends is a very good thing. Through your affection for them you learn to set aside your own narrow self-interest and get a sense of yourself as being involved with other

people in a real and tangible sense. But your family, your circle
of friends, the supporters of your football team, the members of
your ethnic or cultural group, are only a tiny fraction of the universe of living beings. What might it be like to feel the same
warmth towards everyone you meet, whether known to you or
not? This may seem a naive dream, a well-meaning fantasy that
could never be realized, but before we give up the whole idea,
we could consider the implications of one of the essential tenets
of Buddhism – that in reality there is no separate self, and that
we are related, directly or indirectly, to everyone else. If we reflect on this, we will come to see that unlimited friendliness is
not a dream at all. It is we who are in a dream when we imagine
that only our close ties with friends and family are important,
while relationships between other families and other groups are
of little or no consequence.

When we look at things in this way, we have to admit that our
relationships contain more than a little self-interest. Indeed, the
very warmth of our relationships with family members and
close friends can be what makes the rest of the world seem cold,
unfriendly, and uninteresting. Through our relationships we
are seeking security; we want things to stay the same; we want
the relationships we build to provide a refuge against the difficulties and uncertainties of life, thus guaranteeing the stability
and security of our own small, inward-looking world. We need
those people, those relationships, if we are not to feel terribly
alone and vulnerable. We are, in other words, desperately
attached to them, an attachment that is entirely bound up with
pema.

Pema is essentially a social emotion, concerned with preserv-
ing the human group, rather than with transcending boundaries
and reaching out to all life however it manifests. If pema is love
or friendliness that expresses attachment, mettā is love or
friendliness that is not self-referential at all. Both are positive in

their own way, but mettā is positive in the spiritual sense whereas pema is a more worldly emotion. Pema is love and affection for others in the ordinary, human way, ranging from erotic desire to a simple warm fellow feeling, a sense of human solidarity with others.

Pema provides a useful contrast with mettā, as the two words are close enough in meaning to be confused with each other, so that pema is sometimes identified as the 'near enemy' of mettā. Mettā is much more than the warmth of good fellowship, or a gregarious feeling of togetherness. Unlike pema, mettā includes no attachment, no self-interest, no need even to be near its object, much less to possess it. Mettā is not necessarily a reciprocal emotion. As already mentioned, you can cultivate mettā or friendliness towards someone without that person knowing about it – indeed, without your having any connection with them at all. You can even express your mettā in practical ways – by putting in a good word for someone, say, or helping them financially – without there being any personal contact between you.

Ordinarily we feel affection more or less exclusively. Indeed, the more intense the affection, the more exclusive it tends to be. When we use the word 'love' to describe our strong feeling for someone, the someone in question is usually just that – some one: a single individual. It is a strong partiality for that one person over anyone else. But when you feel mettā, a strongly developed feeling of good will towards one person will tend to spread more and more widely. Being without self-interest, mettā is impartial. Just as the sun is not selective in the giving of its light and warmth, when you feel mettā, you don't choose its recipients or keep it for those you deem worthy of it. Mettā is love that breaks out of the narrow confines of self-referential selectivity, love that does not have a preference, non-exclusive love.

If we are going to use the word 'love' at all, we could describe
mettā as disinterested love. It is of course 'interested' in the
sense of 'concerned' – it is not *un*interested – but it is *dis*interested in the sense that when you feel it you have no thought of
what you might get back in return. There are a number of
English words that include a quality of disinterested love or
appreciation in their meaning. Philosophy, for example, is the
love of wisdom for its own sake, not for what is to be gained from
it. Wisdom is essentially useless. Whatever practical purpose it
might have is incidental to what it is really about: the direct realization of the truth of things. Similarly, mettā is concerned with
its object purely for the sake of that object in itself.

There is in mettā no desire to impress, or to ingratiate oneself,
or to feather one's nest, or to gain favours. Nor is there any
expectation of emotional reciprocity. Being friendly or offering
friendship to someone in the spirit of mettā is something you do
for their sake, not just for yours. Mettā is not erotic love, or
parental love, or the love that seeks the admiration and esteem
of a particular social group. It is a cherishing, protecting, matur-
ing love which has the same kind of effect on the spiritual being
of others as the light and heat of the sun have on their physical
being. We really can learn to love in this way. This is the value,
and the challenge, of the third stage of the mettā bhāvanā.

DOING THE METTĀ BHĀVANĀ
FOURTH STAGE: FEELING METTĀ FOR AN ENEMY

*In this stage of the practice you try to make that person
the object of your mettā not on account of anything they
have done or not done but simply because they are there.*

We have already seen that to practise the mettā bhāvanā effectively we need to learn to detach the emotion of which we have

become aware from the person towards whom we are feeling it. Success in the meditation depends in large measure on how pliant one's mind can be in this respect. You probably won't be able to do it straightaway; it takes quite a lot of practice. The challenge is particularly great in the fourth stage of the meditation, when we try to maintain our feelings of loving-kindness in the 'presence' of someone who is perhaps intent on doing us harm.

The method of the mettā bhāvanā is systematically to coax the habitual reactive mind into the first glimmerings of positive emotion by concentrating one's thoughts and emotions on real individuals, with all their virtues and failings. However, sooner or later you will have to detach the emotion from these particular individuals. Mettā is essentially objectless, and in the course of the practice it should come to depend less and less on the nature of the object and more and more on itself. This is what it means to say that mettā is ultimately impersonal. It is no less an emotion, but it is less dependent on particular persons. You feel the same mettā, the same emotional response, towards the so-called enemy as towards the so-called friend.

This does not mean eradicating the particularity of our emotions. Mettā expresses itself in different ways according to the differing nature and degrees of intimacy of our different relationships. What mettā does is infuse our positivity with the heightened energy that previously arose when we felt anger or hatred towards an enemy. The mettā bhāvanā is fundamentally a practice of transformation, not annihilation; the aim is not so much to obliterate our negative emotions as to redirect them. There is energy in anger, and if we are to attain the ultimate good – Nirvāṇa – all our energies, all our emotions, positive and not so positive, have to be released in the direction of that goal. Rather than suppress negative emotions when we can and allow them to run riot when we can't, the aim is to transform the energy in them and integrate it into the existing stream of our positive emotion, thereby making that positive stream of emotion stronger.

Here again there is an important role for reflection, as Śāntideva advises in his *Bodhicaryāvatāra* or 'Guide to the Bodhisattva's Way of Life'. Reminding us of the central Buddhist insight of conditionality, he points out that people who do us harm do so on the basis of conditioning factors over which they have no control: 'A person does not get angry at will, having decided "I shall get angry."' Anger and hatred arise owing to factors outside our conscious control, and the anger with which we respond to anger is also irrational. There is no justification for anger, and no point to it. Anger and hatred are states of suffering that can lead only to further distress, so there is nothing to be gained from perpetuating them. Śāntideva goes on to encourage us to reflect on the painful consequences of our anger or hatred, and to inform our emotional life with the only rational conclusion to draw from these reflections: that unhelpful emotions should be abandoned for more positive ones. This is the only effective way to help beings, including ourselves.

Such reflections may help a little, but our emotions are rarely susceptible to reason alone. It is relatively easy to acknowledge that we feel ill will, and certainly easy to talk about turning it into love, but it is not at all easy actually to bring about the transformation. If the kind of reasoning that Śāntideva proposes is to be successful, we need to ensure that *all* our emotions are lined up behind our spiritual aspirations. If they aren't, anger and hatred, for example, will make their presence felt in a way that obstructs those aspirations (in the guise of 'righteous indignation', for example). We may then find that we simply cannot get started on feeling mettā for our enemy.

It is an unfortunate fact that our emotional life very often tends to lag some way behind our intellectual development. We can analyse our situation indefinitely, but without a fair degree of self-knowledge our feelings will tend to remain tied to their old familiar objects in an ever-recurring cycle of craving and dissatisfaction. Directed thinking is important – indeed, essential – but we also need to find a way of working directly on and with our emotions. Our task is to unlock the energy uselessly tied up in harmful feelings and channel it into positive and productive mental states.

If the object of your attention brings up intensely negative feelings, it can be difficult to get any grip on mettā at all. Positive emotion no longer seems even a remote possibility; just for that moment you seem to have forgotten what mettā might even feel like. If you are beset by strong feelings of resentment, anger, jealousy, or craving, you may feel they are just too much for you to handle at present. If you have presented your emotional positivity with too great a challenge, it may be best to withdraw temporarily and retrace your steps, dwelling for a while longer on someone towards whom your feelings are more straightforwardly positive before returning to this most difficult but vital stage.

We need to be able somehow to grapple with the very idea we have of this person as an 'enemy'. We have probably designated them as such because they have upset us in some way, and now we are maintaining this fixed view of them by dwelling on the injury they have done to us. The solution is simple: concentrate on their more attractive qualities. In order to draw your attention away from someone's irritating habit of always arriving late, for example, you can direct it towards some mitigating factor you have overlooked: they may be turning up late because they are devoted to looking after their young family, for example. You focus on their positive human qualities, or at least the problems which they face. At the very least, you can reflect that they are not always performing injurious actions, or perhaps not towards everybody. In this way you learn to paddle against the stream of your ill will.

You can even begin to like your enemy, just a little. But while such a shift in your feelings is a very positive development, it should not be taken for the arising of mettā itself. Liking someone is not the same as feeling mettā for them. Our usual attitude towards someone perceived to have harmed us – which is what an 'enemy' is by definition – is to feel hatred towards them. But in this stage of the practice you try to make that person the object of your mettā, not on account of anything they have done or not done but simply because they are there. Irrespective of whoever is around, or whether there is anyone around at all, you are aiming to be entirely equanimous in your attitude of loving-kindness. You are not so much feeling love for your enemy as simply being undisturbed in your attitude of mettā towards all beings by the thought of someone who has done you an injury.

Although mettā is in a sense the rational response to reality, in the end it is produced without cause or justification. When we practise the mettā bhāvanā, our feelings of good will towards beings do not arise on account of anything those beings may have said or done. We simply wish them well. If it were otherwise, mettā would be no more than a psychological thing, coming and going in dependence on whom we bring to mind at any one time. As a spiritual quality, mettā is not bound by any kind of stipulation or qualification or condition. It is not meted out according to whether beings deserve it or not.

According to Buddhism, there is no entity corresponding to an unchanging self underlying all that we do and say and experience. If there were, then one might approach the fourth stage of the mettā bhāvanā with the thought that underneath all the bad that one can see in someone, there is something good that is still lovable. To view a person as essentially good despite their unskilful actions suggests there is an underlying person there to begin with. Buddhism, on the other hand, sees a person not as an entity that can become sullied by unskilfulness and then cleansed of impurities, but as the sum total, and nothing more than the sum total, of their actions, bodily, verbal, and mental.

If we are trying to direct loving-kindness towards somebody of whose actions we do not approve, what is it, then, towards which we are really directing our attention? As far as Buddhism is concerned, a person is not any kind of fixed identity. There is no underlying 'self' that is somehow capable of performing actions while remaining essentially unchanged. Those actions are precisely what that human being ultimately is. Hence it is self-contradictory to speak, for example, of hating a person's actions but not the actual person, because the person includes the action that you have just said you condemn. The villain of Shakespeare's *Measure for Measure*, Angelo, who asks with rhetorical sarcasm, 'Condemn the fault and not the actor of it?' is quite right. It cannot be done.

In this penultimate stage of the mettā bhāvanā, you deliber-ately call to mind someone who has hurt you, not in order to change your opinion of them but to test and strengthen your attitude of mettā. If your mettā is genuine, it will not be dis-turbed even by your thinking of a so-called enemy. Taking in their bad qualities with their good qualities, you direct mettā to the person as a whole, good and bad.

This is very much the sense in which we speak of the limitless compassion of the Buddhas towards living beings. A Buddha's compassion – which is the response of mettā to suffering – does not emerge in the form of isolated acts of loving-kindness that you somehow earn by your devotion or some other 'deserving' action. A Buddha has the same attitude of mettā towards beings whatever they do or don't do, because that mettā is beyond time and space; it exists both before and after those beings committed any action or exhibited any quality, skilful or unskilful. This is not to say that Buddhas condone unskilfulness, only that their mettā is unaffected by it and they do not threaten to withdraw their limitless care and concern. Indeed, as it is limitless, you will not get more of it by behaving better. A Buddha's mettā is rather like that of a loyal friend whose attitude does not change even though you have done something to upset them. You may apologize to your friend and beg forgiveness, but they will continue to feel – and perhaps say – that there is nothing to forgive.

The mettā of the Buddhas is unwavering; they are entirely compassionate, before, during, and after whatever might have taken place. For this reason we need never approach them with the slightest fear or apprehension. To sit in judgement forms no part of a Buddha's business. Nor therefore is there any need for us to ask for their forgiveness or mercy. Buddhas do not, after all, administer the law of karma. Conditionality will go on operating, come what may, and nobody, not even a Buddha, can save us from experiencing the consequences of our foolish actions.

The unconditional love of a Buddha takes place on a plane altogether beyond such concepts as 'enemy' or 'person' in the way these terms are generally understood. You can love someone unconditionally, as a Buddha does, only in so far as you believe, unconditionally, that they can change, however apparently hopeless the state they are in. This means being unconditionally willing to help them evolve, irrespective of the point at which they have now arrived. If they have abused you, you fully take in what they have done and still you wish them well. Truly loving someone does not mean seeing them as perfect or their moral weaknesses as unimportant. Quite the opposite: the more you care about someone the more you are concerned for their spiritual welfare. With the warm and unflinching gaze of mettā you see them as they are, warts and all.

Chapter Four

THE CULMINATION
OF METTĀ

Just as a mother would protect her only child at the risk of her own life, even so, let him cultivate a boundless heart towards all beings.

Mātā yathā niyaṃ puttaṃ
āyusā ekaputtam anurakkhe
evam pi sabbabhūtesu
mānasam bhāvaye aparimāṇaṃ.

HOW MUCH METTĀ?

So here we are, poised at the beginning of the fifth stage of the practice, about to gradually extend our mettā beyond all bounds. It seems an appropriate point at which to bring in the next verse of the *Karaṇīya Metta Sutta*, in order to strengthen our sense of the kind of emotional depth we are aspiring to develop. This verse seeks to give us an idea of this, by means of the analogy of a mother's love for her only child. It is an image that seems to stand out from the rest of the sutta, communicating the kind of commitment with which you develop the 'boundless heart', the 'limitless mind', towards all beings. It is a compelling image, although this translation mutes somewhat the full force of the original verse. The Pali words are more emphatic, repeating the word for child, *putta*: 'her child, her only child', to show us the picture of the loving mother concentrated on a single, utterly vulnerable human being. It is a deliberate paradox: the intensity of such love directed towards one person turned outwards to shine upon all living beings.

Maternal love is a particularly appropriate image for mettā, not so much because it is a stronger love than other kinds – romantic love, for instance, can be very powerful – but because it is nurturing love. The love of a mother is concerned to help a child grow and thrive, and mettā has the same quality of support and tender care. A mother seeks her child's well-being in every possible way, preparing and educating them to grow and become strong, healthy, and fulfilled. In the same way, mettā seeks to nurture all living beings, seeking their welfare, wanting to help them to be happy and fulfilled.

A mother will lay down her own life for her child, and mettā is imbued with the same spirit of selflessness, though obviously to go as far as to sacrifice your life for another is the tallest of tall orders. Making that sacrifice on the basis of mettā would not betray a lack of care for yourself, but would express the value you placed on your own potential for future growth (the future as far as you yourself were concerned being a future life, obviously). You cannot truly value yourself as long as you persist in putting yourself before others. To counteract this tendency you may need to make a point of putting others before you, but the aim of this is to value others *as* yourself, not more than yourself.

The quality of impartiality in mettā has a degree of wisdom in it. It is a kind of equanimity that enables you to be quite unbiased in your appreciation of a situation. It has a touch of the objectivity and selflessness of Insight. If you see that the best outcome for everyone might involve a risk to your own life, then you are happy to take that risk. Buddhaghosa gives an illustration of this in his *Visuddhimagga*, or 'Path of Purity'. You are to imagine that you, your best friend, a 'neutral person', and an adversary are held up by bandits while travelling, and the bandits offer to spare the lives of just three of you. It is up to you to choose which one of you is to be sacrificed. Buddhaghosa says that if you had developed perfect equanimity, you would be unable to express a preference. You wouldn't automatically opt to save yourself, but neither would you automatically offer to give up your own life. You would consider the situation with an even mind, no less concerned for the fate of others than for your own. This is equanimity, an attitude that in its profound objectivity values all – including one's own self – equally highly.

As well as being self-sacrificing, the love of a mother also involves a willingness to take responsibility for her children. The gratitude we feel towards our mother is for the affection she has given us but also for the fact that she has taken responsibility for us: she has thought for us, planned for us, taken our long-term needs into consideration before we had any idea of what we would need to get through life. The role of thinking for others that a mother assumes for her children is also taken by other people in our lives: nurses and doctors, for example, have to ensure their patients' needs are met, whether or not the patients themselves know what those needs are. Medical professionals make it their business to be aware of the medical conditions that affect their patients and take responsibility for guiding their recovery. It is a kind of compassion that includes an intelligent objectivity. The same objectivity is found in mettā.

If you really seek the good of others, you must have an understanding of what that good actually is. If you do not, you may turn into a do-gooder, relentlessly interfering in people's lives in a way that involves no awareness of their wishes and needs, however helpful and benevolent you may wish to appear. For an example of this sort of thing I'm afraid I must fall back on the old joke about the Boy Scout who reports that he has done his good deed for the day by helping an old lady across the road. 'That doesn't sound very difficult,' says the Scout leader. 'Oh yes it was,' replies the boy, 'She didn't want to cross.' Good intentions alone are not enough, and even the well-intentioned love of a mother is not infallible, although her instincts are usually reliable enough. Likewise, the objective intelligence of mettā, if it involves some element of Insight or wisdom, is intuitive in its own way – intuitive, not thoughtless.

Mettā is like a mother's love in that it is intense, selfless, nurturing, and even intuitive. But it is quite unlike the mother's love in one crucial respect: a mother's love – perhaps especially if she has only one child – is limited to her own offspring, whereas mettā is universal and unlimited. A mother views her child as a kind of extension of her own being, and it is as natural for her to love her baby as it is for her to love herself. But that does not constitute a real transcendence of self, because the scope of her intense concern is so circumscribed.

The expression of mettā certainly does not involve smothering people with sticky affection or drawing them into a dependent relationship. A mother's love may even cause her to act unskilfully for the benefit of her own child, even at the expense of others. She may, for example, become fanatically competitive on behalf of her family, with ruthless disregard for the well-being of other children. A mother is fierce in defending her young, but when it comes to encouraging the child to become a person in his or her own right, mother-love can hinder the child's development and place unnecessary obstacles in the way of their emerging individuality. Of course, a mother may feel, or develop, mettā towards her children, as indeed may a father.

From an Enlightened point of view, all beings are helpless. However capable they may be in mundane matters, spiritually speaking they are like helpless children. In this sense a Buddha or a Bodhisattva is very much like a mother, helping beings to grow up spiritually. But the analogy of the mother's love is no more than an analogy. Mettā is in some ways quite different from maternal affection. It is perhaps significant that the verse following the analogy with the love of a mother for her only child should emphasize the unbounded quality of mettā. It is as though the possibility of misunderstanding the analogy has been anticipated, and the qualities of mettā that a mother's love does not necessarily share have been brought quickly forward to guard against such a possibility.

*Let his thoughts of boundless love pervade
the whole world: above, below and across
without any obstruction, without any hatred,
without any enmity.*

*Mettañ ca sabbalokasmiṃ
mānasam bhāvaye aparimāṇaṃ
uddhaṃ adho ca tiriyañ ca
asambādhaṃ averaṃ asapattaṃ.*

METTĀ FOR ALL BEINGS

The Pali phrase translated here as 'without any enmity' can be
translated more literally and precisely as 'without any enemy'.
This is a subtle difference, but significant in that if you declare
yourself to be 'without any enemy' you are in effect saying that
you regard nobody as being beyond the reach of your good will.

In the fifth stage of the mettā bhāvanā we try to remove the
barriers we habitually raise between ourselves and others by
extending an equal concern and regard towards ourselves, our
friend, the neutral person, and the enemy. Then we extend our
mettā beyond these individuals to encompass all beings everywhere. This idea of 'all beings' is not meant to refer to a finite and
limited number of beings, but at the same time we can't really
conceive of there being an unlimited number of beings. If this
seems like a dilemma, the nature of mettā supplies the solution.
Mettā cannot settle down and stop at a given number of beings.
Your benevolence and compassion continuously expands, taking in more and more people all the time. The natural tendency
of the mind is to set limits and settle down, but positive emotion
goes against this tendency.

This is especially clear at the beginning of the last stage of the
mettā bhāvanā meditation when, having equalized your loving-
kindness towards the four individuals from each of the previous

stages, you allow your mettā to open out completely, to become free of any specific reference. You no longer consider individual beings, but the mettā goes on, and as your thoughts fall on each person the mettā naturally expresses itself towards them. Outside the context of meditation, too, your mettā will have no particular object, but as you encounter individuals it will express itself in your feeling and behaviour towards them.

Mettā is ultimately a state of mind or heart. This means that in the final stage of the mettā bhāvanā, although you may be concentrating now on this, now on that aspect of the totality of living beings, your attention, your concentration, remains constant. Although you cultivate that state in reference to a specific person or succession of people, once it really starts flowing you don't need to direct it towards anybody in particular. In this respect mettā is like the sun. The sun goes on shining whether or not anything is there to receive its rays. If a planet happens to be in the path of the sun's rays, it is bathed in that light; otherwise, the sunlight just continues to stream through space. In the same way, if someone comes into the orbit of your mettā, your mettā falls upon them. If no one is there to receive it, mettā just carries on infinitely throughout space, as it were.

Thus, strictly speaking, it is not that you *direct* mettā towards someone. Nor do you literally imagine all the beings in the world in front of you and make them the collective object of your mettā. Nor can you possibly be aware of every one of them individually. But there is an infinitely expanding flow of mettā that goes on and on, arising and expanding, and anyone who comes into your mind is lit up by its warmth and brightness. Looking at it in this way, we can begin to form an idea of mettā not so much as a state of mind, but as a movement within consciousness, or a medium within which consciousness can move.

Clearly it is too much to expect that your positive emotion will be universal and unlimited at the outset. This is a progressive practice of cultivation, not instant Enlightenment. But your developing experience of mettā, if it really is mettā, will show in a tendency to become more and more inclusive of others, and less and less tied to your own narrow interests. The seed of Buddhahood is there in every small, everyday thought or word of generosity or act of friendliness. Indeed, this naturally expansive, other-regarding tendency is the quality common to all truly positive emotions, whereas negativity shuts us down, closes us in upon the private, self-regarding 'I'.

THE IMMEASURABLES
If it really is mettā you are feeling, you will never feel you have had enough.

The first four stages of the mettā bhāvanā are there to help you get the mettā flowing. Once it is in full flow, you can let it spread in any direction you like, strengthening it and extending its flow more and more widely. You can send it in the direction of animals, towards sick people, old people, famine victims, evil dictators, wherever your thoughts take you.

The same goes for the other brahma vihāra meditations: the *karuṇā bhāvanā* or development of compassion, the *muditā bhāvanā* or cultivation of sympathetic joy, and the *upekkhā bhāvanā* (*upekṣā* in Sanskrit) or cultivation of equanimity. Each of them shares with mettā the same limitless object. This is perhaps most obvious with upekkhā or equanimity. To speak of an equanimity that is somehow restricted to a few people would be a contradiction, because the essential nature of equanimity is to not make distinctions but to have an even mind towards all.

The brahma vihāras are all closely interconnected. Indeed the basic emotional state underlying them all is the same: it is mettā. If you experience mettā and that mettā encounters someone who is happy, it is transformed into sympathetic joy, muditā, the state of being happy in the happiness of others, rejoicing in their merits and positive qualities. The inherently outgoing quality of muditā reaches its peak when you are able to recognize and rejoice in the merits of people who perform positive actions even when they seem to be set against you. You are still as happy to rejoice in their merits as in the merits of your friends.

If you could appreciate only the skilful actions of people you liked, or who liked you, this would be a very limited form of muditā, and if you could appreciate only those actions that benefited or gratified you in some way, muditā would not come into it at all. Muditā is the appreciation of the true happiness of others. If you can't rejoice with others, if you can't feel happiness in their happiness, then you can have no real mettā for them.

But suppose your mettā encounters someone who is suffering. Mettā is then transformed into karuṇā, the strong and practical desire to do whatever one can to relieve suffering. Like muditā, upekkhā, and mettā, the natural tendency of compassion is to reach out and to go on expanding its field of activity ever further and more powerfully. Indeed, any positive emotion has this tendency. We look upon not just one person, but anyone we meet, with the love a mother feels for her own helpless child. All the time the same light of mettā is shining through. Then, according to whether people suffer or whether they are happy, this same basic positive emotional attitude will be mantled with the sober shades of karuṇā or clothed in the bright, dancing colours of muditā.

To the four brahma vihāras one could arguably add other positive mental states which have become non-exclusive and expansive, which as positive mental states they will indeed do. Devotion, for example, might appear to be necessarily limited and exclusive in its frame of reference, but this is not really the case. Devotion is the emotion that arises when our mettā touches upon something much higher and nobler than ourselves. When you look up with love, your love becomes reverence and devotion – *śraddhā* and *bhakti*, to use the Sanskrit terms. Conversely, the mettā of the Buddhas looking upon all beings who are not yet Enlightened of course becomes karuṇā, compassion.

Devotion in Buddhism is usually considered in terms of the Indian idea of *bhakti*, the pleasure felt in connection with the contemplation of spiritual objects. Although this plays its part in Buddhist devotion, it is not really about showing formal respect towards the symbols of religious authority. It is an aspect of faith, and includes a degree of certainty that the path you follow is the sure path to your goal, your ultimate good. It contains a strong element of insight, the direct knowledge that certain practices will lead to certain results.

As a Buddhist you are drawn to the Buddha, the Dharma, and the Sangha, confident that these represent the ultimate values of life, that they symbolize humanity's highest goal. Being intent upon the Three Jewels in this way brings a clarity to the mind over and above whatever pleasure you may or may not feel. To be devoted in the true sense is to acknowledge and to resonate spiritually with any representation of your goal. If devotion is limited to only some of its forms – those exclusively connected with a certain school of Buddhism, for example – it is scarcely devotion in the true sense. Even though the images as cultural objects may not be familiar, or even particularly attractive, the devoted Buddhist still recognizes in them the goal that is common to all Buddhists. This is because the goal itself is beyond language, beyond culture. It does not find full expression in any particular set of forms.

Positive emotion, whether it is devotion or mettā or anything else, is expansive by its very nature. If one's sense of devotion is not broadening its scope, it is thus not really a positive emotion at all. Like mettā, its tendency is to become universal. Mettā should go on expanding, renewing itself, growing brighter and stronger as it does so. If it really is mettā you are feeling, you will never feel you have had enough.

Whether he stands, walks, sits or lies down,
as long as he is awake, he should develop
this mindfulness. This they say is the
noblest living here.

Tiṭṭham caraṃ nisinno vā
sayāno vā yāvat' assa vigatamiddho
etaṃ satiṃ adhiṭṭheyya;
brahmam etaṃ vihāraṃ idha-m-āhu.

HOW YOUR METTĀ AFFECTS OTHERS

Of course, mettā is not just a meditation exercise; it's a way of life. The phrase 'whether he stands, walks, sits or lies down' is found in almost identical form in the verse on mindfulness of the body in the *Satipaṭṭhāna Sutta*, the discourse on the four foundations of mindfulness. Like mindfulness, mettā is something you never lose sight of, and clearly this verse of the sutta envisages it as a form of mindfulness. If you really want to attain the 'noblest living', you will need to practise mettā in every moment of the day and night, not just when you are seated on your meditation cushion. This is mettā in the full or true sense.

The qualifier 'as long as he is awake' can be taken in different ways. It refers to being awake in the everyday sense, but if you are going to be truly awake in the sense of *sati*, mindfulness, then you can take such wakefulness in connection with mettā into your dream life. In fact, in any state of consciousness, mettā will stand you in good stead, as long as you remain attentive. So the phrase can refer to a physical state or a spiritual state, but it can also refer to a more general state of alertness or vigour.

Etaṃ satiṃ adhiṭṭheyya, which Saddhatissa translates as 'let him develop this mindfulness', could perhaps also be rendered as 'let him radiate this mindfulness', implying that by this stage of the sutta you are no longer in the process of developing the 'power' of mettā. That power has now been developed, and you are just extending its influence, radiating mettā for the benefit of all beings everywhere.

But while your mettā may have a powerful influence on others, an influence that you are now able to extend and to radiate, it is in no sense your own. We do speak of 'developing' mettā, but this is not a kind of power technique whose aim is to manipulate other people to one's own advantage. Mettā is certainly powerful, but it is not a coercive power. For example, if you cultivate mettā towards an 'enemy', there is at least a possibility that this will have a positive effect on their behaviour towards you, but you are not to think of mettā as a force or power, to be used so that others will have no choice but to fall under your spell and like you. This would not be mettā, but an assertion of your ego over that of another person. It is of course skilful to direct mettā towards people who seem to be trying to do us harm. But if we do so just to stop them giving us a difficult time and making a nuisance of themselves, it probably won't be the real thing. If we then start getting irritated because we have tried to be full of mettā towards them and they do not respond positively, then our mental state will be not unlike theirs.

Other factors being equal, your practice of the mettā bhāvanā will have a positive effect on others. The expansive quality of mettā is by no means confined to meditation. One of the sure signs of mettā is that you will quite naturally have a lightening, encouraging, even tonic effect on those around you. But others must be allowed the freedom to resist that influence if they want to. In the end we are all responsible for our own mental state. A positive emotion cannot be imposed.

There is also the possibility that some people may not be sensitive to your mettā, particularly if they are used to relationships based on a kind of emotional quid pro quo, in which everything one is given has to be paid for. Mettā is entirely unconditional, and when people are used to emotional dependency in a relationship, they may think you are rather uninterested in them, or even that you don't care about them, simply because you seem not to want anything from them in return. The mettā coming from you is a little too rarefied; it isn't quite on their wavelength. Even though you may be clearly concerned for their welfare, good will is not what they want: they want some kind of commitment and surrender, some dependency, to fill the aching void left by their incapacity to feel mettā towards themselves. Your mettā may mean very little to them if they interpret your unwillingness to enter into a dependent relationship as meaning that you are rather distant and impersonal.

The idea that mettā is something expansive comes through again in the last line of the verse, in the expression *Brahmam etaṃ vihāraṃ*. Here, the word *vihāraṃ* means 'abode', 'state', or 'experience', while *brahmam* means 'high', 'noble', 'sublime' – exalted, that is to say, almost to the point of divinity. According to some authorities, the word *brahman* comes from a root meaning to swell, grow, or expand. The brahmin was thus originally the inspired sage, the priest or holy man who, having 'swelled' under the pressure of divine inspiration, released it to the community as holy teachings. So *brahmam* is something divinely great in the sense of 'expanded', and in this way comes to approximate to the idea of 'the absolute'.

Idha-m-āhu – 'This, they say' – comes at the end of the verse as a further clue as to how we should understand *brahmam vihāraṃ*. It is as though this expression, although it describes the ultimate outcome of the training, is, in the final analysis, only a figure of speech. The experience is ineffable, so to call it 'the Sublime Abiding' is only a metaphor, a poetic turn of phrase. There is, however, no implication of any kind of doubt or disclaimer: rather the opposite. It is affirming that this is not just personal experience, but the experience of many others. It is an appeal to tradition, in other words, to the experience and testimony of the spiritual community of those who are truly wise.

Just as a mother's nurturing love for her child helps the child to grow, our mettā for others helps them to develop, as well as being the means of our own growth and development. Mettā is not only expansive in itself; it is also a cause of increase and expansion in others, and of the joy that comes with such expansion. It brings a lightness to your being, taking you beyond narrow, purely personal concerns. You start to become receptive to other people, happy to open yourself up and let them in, unafraid to pay them more attention and give them more of yourself.

Mettā is not just metaphorically expansive. You *feel* expansive; you feel an airy and weightless joy. This quality is characteristic of positive emotion generally, hence expressions like 'up in the clouds' and 'walking on air', and mettā is the brightest and most positive of emotional states. You feel carried outside yourself, warm, sunny, uplifted. If you want to develop the joy of mettā, look for this sense of lightness. If your devotions are heavy and cheerless, and your faith is a dull and dismal piety, mettā, which has the taste of freedom and delight, will be very slow in coming.

Of course, freedom and delight are not emotions usually associated with religion, especially in Europe, where an uplifting legacy of tapering Gothic spires and sublime church music is accompanied by the whiff of brimstone and the promise of eternal damnation for the unbeliever. Anxiety and guilt may be the traditional flavours of established religion in our culture, but they are the antithesis of mettā. It is a dreadful pity that our emotions are so often a source of misery rather than joy. No wonder that we try to suppress, constrict, and crush them! But in doing so, we compound our unhappiness. We become more and more downcast, we go about with head bowed and shoulders drooping, and of course it spreads. When we meet someone who starts to tell us about their difficulties, we can't wait to start putting in a word about our own troubles, looking for an audience for our complaints.

But just as we tend to want to pass on our misery, the generosity of spirit that comes with mettā makes us want to confer our happiness on everyone we meet. While intention is the starting point of mettā, its culmination is a matter of conduct, the 'noblest living' of Saddhatissa's translation.

FRIENDLINESS AND FRIENDSHIP
If you never experience mettā in the closeness and reciprocity of friendships that are essentially spiritual rather than collusive, you will never experience the full possibilities of mettā.... It is very difficult to develop mettā as a purely individual experience. You need other people.

No doubt if everyone in the world were to cultivate genuinely expansive positive emotion as a way of life, human society would be entirely transformed. But even though this is hardly feasible, at least for the time being, it should be possible to experience such a thing within the sangha, the spiritual community. The sangha is the expression, across time and space, of that practical commitment to transforming self and world which is inherent in the life and teaching of the Buddha. Through kalyāṇa mitratā, or spiritual friendship, through which one connects with and encourages the best in one's friends, one generates and intensifies positive emotions in a continual reciprocity of good will.

In the sangha, everyone is committed to the cultivation of mettā as a way of life, mettā being experienced as a practical reality through friendship. You may well profess great feelings of mettā towards all sentient beings, and even perhaps try to put mettā into practice in the way you behave with colleagues and acquaintances. But how far are you really living out your ideals? If you never experience mettā in the closeness and reciprocity of friendships that are essentially spiritual rather than collusive, you will never experience the full possibilities of mettā. Spiritual friendship enables us to be true to our individuality and on that basis bring about an authentic meeting of hearts and minds. It is very difficult to develop mettā as a purely individual experience. You need other people.

Conclusion

THE REALIZATION
OF METTĀ

Not falling into wrong views, being virtuous and endowed with insight, by discarding attachment to sense desires, never again is he reborn.

Diṭṭhiñ ca anupagamma
sīlavā dassanena sampanno
kāmesu vineyya gedhaṃ
na hi jātu gabbhaseyyaṃ punar eti.

A FINGER POINTING TO THE MOON

The opening verses of the sutta laid down the necessary foundations of the practice. Now the closing verse describes the results of one's perfecting it. The term *dassanena*, translated here as 'insight', is more literally 'sight' or 'vision', as in 'seeing the true nature of things'. Both *dassana* and the first word of this verse, *diṭṭhiñ*, come from the same root: *diṭṭhi* (*dṛṣṭi* in Sanskrit), which means 'view', commonly occurring in the expressions *micchā diṭṭhi*, 'wrong view', and *sammā diṭṭhi*, 'right view'. Whereas *dassana*, like vision, the English equivalent, always has positive connotations, *diṭṭhi*, views, can be positive or negative depending on how it is qualified. However, the word *diṭṭhi* on its own, without a qualifier, is always negative. It is understandable, therefore, that this phrase has been translated as 'falling into wrong views' – but this does change the meaning. The implication of the Pali word is not only that one should avoid falling into wrong views, but that any view at all ultimately gets in the way of true Insight. Even right views are to be given up eventually, in the sense that, though still holding them, one is not attached to them.

By 'view' is meant any conceptual formulation to which you adhere as if it had absolute value as a truth-statement. 'I exist' is a view, and so is 'the moon is in the sky.' Such views are necessary for communication, and conventionally speaking we need to label some as true and some as false. From the point of view of the Dharma, too, we need to distinguish between views that are helpful to the attainment of our goal and those that point us in the wrong direction, spiritually speaking. But from the point of view of the goal, reality itself, all views are inadequate. No view is capable of expressing that reality. They are expedient means, only representations of things, not the truth.

Thus, on many occasions, not only in the Pali scriptures but also in the Mahāyāna sūtras, the Buddha states that the Tathāgata (another term for Buddha) is free from all views. Even though he spent some forty years treading the roads of ancient India, giving discourses, making careful distinctions between right views and wrong views, in reality, as a Buddha, he has no views.

This paradox reminds us that we need to hold our views lightly. As the Zen tradition puts it, they are a finger pointing to the moon, not the moon itself. The Buddha uses words like 'self', 'person', and 'Enlightenment', for example, but he doesn't have a view of self, or person, or Enlightenment; that is, he doesn't adhere to any conceptual formulation of any kind as having absolute validity. Not falling into views means not 'absolutizing' any conceptual construction. However useful a set of concepts might be for the purposes of communication, if you adhere to them as anything more than useful markers, you have fallen into a kind of literalism, or even fundamentalism. Any concept relies for its meaning on its relationship with a whole string of other ideas and concepts which are equally relative. No view, no concept, is independent and therefore fixed. In fact, as soon as you start to take your conceptual constructions too literally, and hold on to them too tightly, they cease to function effectively as a means of communication.

We tend to think of a concept as the content of our communication; it is easily forgotten that it is more fundamentally a *means* of communication. A concept is the means of communicating something that is essentially incommunicable. Concepts do not exist on their own; they come as part of a package that includes the way they are presented. To communicate, they must be offered in the right spirit, at the right time, in the right place, and in the right way. Above all, they have to be put across with the right feeling.

An idea of mettā that lacks the corresponding emotion only muddies the waters when we try to communicate it to others. Indeed, this is true of any Buddhist doctrine. If you want, for example, to communicate the teaching of *anattā* (that there is no unchanging 'self' or 'soul'), you have to be aware that to insist on the idea of no self and argue belligerently, not to say self-assertively, with those who hold a different view undermines the very point you are trying to make. In the name of a view that is meant to pull down the barriers between yourself and others, you are, through your self-assertion, building up those barriers more strongly than ever.

As a Buddhist you need to be familiar with the concept of *anattā*, but you should not cling to any particular formulation of that concept. It is there to be used simply as a vehicle of thought and communication. We need Buddhism as a system of doctrines and practices to be used appropriately, not so that we may have something to hide behind. If you use Buddhism as a collection of ideas to mark you out as a 'spiritual' and perhaps rather interesting or mysterious person, this is at the expense of a deeper emotional engagement with the truth towards which any conceptual formulation can only point. A view of Buddhism, in other words, is an essentially alienated version of Buddhism, and a very different thing from Buddhism itself.

METTĀ AND INSIGHT
At the back of all negative emotion is the thought 'What's in this for me?'

The final words of the sutta – 'never again is he reborn' – suggest that the goal of mettā is a depth of transcendental realization that frees the practitioner from the suffering of repeated rebirth. So how might this be the case? Simply put, in developing mettā, we are deepening our emotional involvement with the truth of anattā or no-self.

The unenlightened person takes the self, specifically their own self, as the fundamental and absolute reality of things, and this has a profoundly negative effect on every aspect of experience. At the back of all negative emotion is the thought 'What's in this for me?' Even in our cultivation of positive emotion, the sense of self acts as a kind of gravitational pull that prevents our reaching the heights to which our mettā would otherwise take us and makes it very difficult for our friendliness and kindness towards others to be truly selfless. Cultivating mettā is like launching a satellite. It may look as though it is tracing a straight line away from the earth into space, but in fact it remains tied to the earth's gravitational field. Rather than disappearing off into the blue, it comes to maintain a steady orbit around the earth, and never fully breaks away.

Mettā behaves similarly. It is inherently expansive, but however strong our feelings of warmth and friendliness, the very fact that we still think of ourselves as separate from others will have a limiting effect on our experience of it. At some point those good intentions reaching out across the universe will start to deviate from their perfectly straight trajectory and slowly curve round, so as not to lose contact with the self entirely. How far your ability to experience genuine mettā carries you before you settle back into a comfortable orbit around the self is a measure of the quality of your practice. The affection between ordinary friends might produce quite a low orbit, while the intimacy and trust of a spiritual friendship would trace out a wider trajectory. The more powerful positive emotion experienced in the deep meditative states called dhyāna would take your course a good deal further out still. Dhyāna is clearly a vast improvement on everyday self-interest; it is a far wider, more elevated reach of consciousness. But however wide its circle of influence may be, it continues to be self-referential, albeit more and more subtly. Only when mettā is permeated by Insight, or a deeper understanding of the truth of anattā, do our emotions finally go beyond the range of the self.

This is of course an analogy. When we practise mettā it isn't that there are literally beams of mettā radiating out from us as we sit and meditate, even though the image might be a useful one. Moreover, that central point of reference, that 'core' of the self, is in reality only a fiction. It is more useful to regard mettā as an outward movement *of* the self rather than *from* the self. As we continually expand the scope of our care and concern, the self is universalized, one might say, or expanded indefinitely. This does not mean that we have to transform our sense of who we *are* according to an idea of how we *should be* that is quite alien to how we experience ourselves. It is rather that our direct experience of ourselves should be that we are continually going out to be aware of and concerned for the well-being of others, not fixed on any single point of identity.

This directly experienced Insight into the truth of no-self (*anattā*) is the first real breakthrough on the journey towards Enlightenment. It is traditionally known as *sotāpatti*, 'entering the stream'. The 'Stream Entrant' is one who has broken the fetter of self-view, who understands directly and intuitively that the separate self, the 'I', is no more than an idea – an idea that is the ultimate source of our unhappiness and lack of fulfilment.

This insight is not merely cognitive, not a matter of intellectual assent to a logical proposition. The Stream Entrant *lives* his or her knowledge, experiencing it in the form of a fully developed positivity. Once one has reached this point, one will never fall back into mistaken, worldly ways, and one will have to undergo no more than seven 're-becomings'.

If we could really see that there is no difference between our own true interests and those of others, mettā would come naturally. As our capacity for positive emotion grows stronger, self-reference becomes ever more difficult to detect, because it becomes harder for us to tell just where the boundaries of the self lie.

The Buddhist tradition offers yet another way of understanding the situation. According to the analytical psychology of the Abhidhamma, while the brahma vihāras are positive and highly skilful mental events, they lack any element of Insight. They are thus classified as *samatha* practices, dedicated to calming and concentrating the mind, rather than as practices devoted to the development of *vipassanā*, or Insight. As such they are mundane (*lokiya*), not transcendental (*lokuttara*), inasmuch as they are temporary emotional states, and cease to exist once the factors that have provided support for them – such as regular meditation, spiritual friendships, study, retreats, and right livelihood – are removed. This said – again according to the Abhidhamma – the brahma vihāras can be transformed by the Insight generated by sustained reflection (itself supported by the basis of samatha that they provide). They will then arise naturally from the clear knowledge that there is no real difference between self and others. But as cultivated states they are not themselves capable of that transformation.

As a result of this kind of analysis, it was said – and perhaps Buddhaghosa bears some responsibility for this – that mettā doesn't take you very far along the path to Enlightenment. The traditional Theravādin view is that you cannot gain Enlightenment by practising the mettā bhāvanā alone, because the mettā bhāvanā is essentially a samatha practice. Indeed, it came as a surprise to me, when I lived among eastern Buddhists, to find that the mettā bhāvanā was often regarded as a simple little practice that anybody could do, two minutes of it at a time being considered more than enough.

The Theravāda's relegation of mettā bhāvanā to the samatha side of things seems to be an example of a general methodological undervaluation of positive emotion, associated with a preference for expressing spiritual perspectives in negative terms. In the Pali canon, and in the Theravādin tradition that is based upon it, Enlightenment is generally spoken of as a state in which the self has been eliminated or – to translate the term *Nibbāna* literally – 'snuffed out'. But in the *Karaṇīya Metta Sutta* the same aim is envisaged in positive terms: not as the elimination of the ego but as a deeply realized attitude of even-mindedness towards all.

There are other sections of the Pali canon that make it abundantly clear that, just as there are negative emotions that bind beings to the wheel of rebirth, there are positive emotions that are not just conducive, but absolutely necessary to the attainment of Insight. Insight is, after all, a realization of – among other things – a state of egolessness, and this is the aim of the mettā bhāvanā. You succeed in the practice of the mettā bhāvanā when in the fifth stage you can genuinely feel equal love towards all. If your care for others is made genuinely equal to your care for yourself, your whole attitude is egoless.

TAKING METTĀ TOWARDS INSIGHT
Realizing the truth of egolessness simply means being truly and deeply unselfish.

The traditional Theravādin attitude rests on the distinction it makes between the emotions and the intellect, with Insight being seen as an essentially intellectual realization. But fully developed mettā is inherently more than an emotion pure and simple, and Insight is inherently more than just cognitive. If your experience of mettā is straightforwardly emotional, and not based on much reflection, then it is the emotional equivalent of Insight, not Insight per se. But even the deepest insight need not be experienced cognitively – that is, it need not take the form of a logical proposition. You simply live it, experience it, as a fully developed positivity and selflessness that is neither emotional nor cognitive.

A common misapprehension is to think of Insight and egolessness in abstract, even metaphysical, terms rather than as comprising concretely-lived attitudes and behaviour. But realizing the truth of egolessness simply means being truly and deeply unselfish. To contemplate the principle of egolessness as some special principle that is somehow separate from our actual behaviour will leave it as far away as ever. If we find it difficult to realize the ultimate emptiness of the self, the solution is to try to be a little less selfish. The understanding comes after the experience, not before.

When it is less than fully developed, mettā may lack the clear awareness that is characteristic of Insight arrived at through reflection on the Dharma. Nonetheless, it is always heading in the direction of a brighter and clearer awareness, as its nature is to grow and expand beyond the limits set by the self. In short, mettā and Insight are not separate aims. Indeed, mettā is a necessary aspect of Insight, and with reflection on the real nature of mettā, Insight will shine through. Having developed mettā in a limited sense as an equal kindness towards others, you can go on to reflect on whether there is really any difference between yourself and others and, if so, what that difference might be. Thus reflecting, you will begin to see that the idea that 'I am I' and 'he is he' is no more than a delusion, and in that way mettā begins to blend with Insight.

It isn't that you drop the mettā in order to start developing Insight. If in the course of your meditation you were to develop mettā, and then were to begin vipassanā-type reflection on that basis, it would represent a continuity of experience, not a shift from one kind of consciousness to another. The Mahāyāna expresses this poetically, saying that the cultivated emotions of the brahma vihāras pass through the fires of *suññatā*, or emptiness – that is, non-self or non-duality – thus giving rise to the *bodhicitta*, or wisdom heart. Of course, in practice one's experience of mettā is likely to flag, to be revived by again bringing to mind and heart other living beings before vipassanā-type reflection is resumed. In this way one's practice alternates between concentration and reflection, samatha and Insight, perhaps for a long time, until eventually the two merge as clear Insight rooted in powerful positive emotion.

It is in terms of Insight that the expansive aspect of mettā, its tendency to break through any sense of exclusivity, is so important – though it is easy to overlook this because mettā has no conceivable end-point. But to miss the link between mettā and Insight is to miss the point of mettā entirely. For example, people sometimes talk about doing things 'for the sake of my spiritual development', which seems a grotesque reduction of any truly spiritual practice, especially in the case of the mettā bhāvanā, mettā being essentially good will that is free from self-interest. That one should aim to develop that disinterested good will in one's own interest clearly undermines the whole enterprise.

While the mettā bhāvanā begins with a cherishing of oneself, this is meant to be the springboard for the practice, not an end in itself. Of course, you do benefit yourself when you help others; even if you give a beggar some money because you think the giving will be good for you, at least you have parted with the money, and both parties are happier as a result. It is difficult to stop yourself from thinking of the ways you are going to benefit from what you do, but you just have to try to focus on your altruistic intention and keep the knowledge of what you will get out of your action in the background, as it were. If you are practising the mettā bhāvanā chiefly for the sake of its beneficial effect on your own mind, that benefit will be diminished, as will any benefit to others, because the practice was vitiated from the outset by self-interest. The more heartfelt your intention to do the mettā bhāvanā entirely for the sake of others, the more beneficial the practice will be, both to you and to them. The idea is gently but persistently to expand the boundaries of your mettā and therewith the boundaries of your own self.

When mettā is experienced in this fully expansive mode and is universal in its scope, there is no experience of a self that is separate from anyone or anything else. To speak of 'oneself' at this stage is almost a contradiction in terms. Just as a circle that has expanded to infinity is not really a circle any more, having gone beyond any distinguishable shape, so the mind that has expanded to embrace all beings has gone beyond definition. Forgetting the self as a reference point, no longer asking what any given situation means for you alone, you can go on indefinitely and happily expanding the breadth and depth of your interest and positivity. The self is replaced by a creative orientation of being, or rather – since 'being' is not a very Buddhistic expression – a creative orientation of becoming.

This is the essence of the spiritual life: to bring about a state in which the whole movement and tendency of our being is expansive, spiralling creatively outwards and upwards. If, on the other hand, we remain fixed in the circularity of reactive consciousness, returning again and again to a fixed and finite idea of the self as the central point of reference, even spiritual achievements can become fetters, by remaining our own 'property'.

Stream Entry – after which, according to tradition, one is not reborn more than seven times – is the point at which the balance of skilful and unskilful energies is decisively shifted towards the positive. Until that point is reached there will always be some degree of conflict between our skilful aspirations and our unskilful resistance to change. For this reason we will sometimes get tired of practising the mettā bhāvanā. But to the extent that we succeed in raising some genuine mettā, it will, we shall find, generate its own energy and expansiveness and depend less on our efforts, at least until we again experience the resistance of some aspect of ourselves that is not behind our skilful intention. Indeed, with repeated application, the mettā we develop will gradually integrate the energy of our resistance into the outward flow of our beneficial energies.

Mettā has the taste of freedom. If you are able to act out of mettā – if you treat others just as you treat yourself – you are acting as if the distinction you unthinkingly create in your mind between yourself and others simply did not exist. In doing so, you free yourself from the power of the illusion of a separate self. This is Insight, and though you might not experience it in a cognitive way, the fact that you have developed mettā, the emotional equivalent of Insight, means that you have developed Insight nonetheless. It is a mistake to approach the practice of the mettā bhāvanā as though it were an elementary exercise, a mere preparation for 'proper' Insight practices. The *Karaṇīya Metta Sutta* is dedicated to a very high ideal: the cultivation of mettā as a path to Insight.

HOW FAR DOES METTĀ GET YOU?

The concluding line of the sutta seems to suggest that the culmination of the perfection of mettā is Enlightenment itself. Taken literally, however, the line does not exclude further re-birth. The text says 'For him there is no re-becoming in any womb (*gabbhaseyyaṃ*),' which would seem conclusive if it were not for the fact that, according to the Buddhist tradition, birth via the womb is not the only possible mode of birth. In fact, four modes – birth from a womb, birth from an egg, birth from mois-ture, and apparitional birth – are mentioned in Buddhist texts of all kinds. So for the traditional Buddhist, although this verse means that they will not be reborn in the human or animal realms, this does not rule out the other three kinds of rebirth. In the higher heavenly worlds, for example, the gods are born by apparitional birth – that is, they just appear – as the result of their previous karma. This is the mode of rebirth of the 'Non-Returner', or *anāgāmin*: he or she is reborn in the Pure Abodes and dwells there surrounded by the golden light of the Buddha's teaching until such time as supreme Enlightenment finally dawns.

This Theravādin doctrine has an approximate parallel in the Mahāyāna Buddhist teaching of the Pure Land, the main differ-ence being that the Bodhisattva may take further rebirth out of compassion, to help beings still suffering in impure realms of existence. The Bodhisattva Kṣitigarbha, for instance, vows to refrain from becoming Enlightened until every region of hell has been emptied of tormented beings. He consciously chooses to be reborn, even though in a sense it is an inevitable choice, flowing naturally from his compassion. Thus, like the Non-Returner, the Bodhisattva does not undergo the involuntary rebirth that con-ditioned beings must endure in consequence of their actions in previous lives.

Whether or not we are prepared to take this distinction be-tween kinds of rebirth as applicable to the text we are studying depends to some extent on how we take the text itself. We can be fairly sure that early on in the transmission of the Buddha's teaching certain expressions will have had a metaphorical rather than a literal significance. Then, as the Abhidharma tradition developed through the centuries, particular terms did come to acquire a more precise meaning. The heaven realms and the different kinds of rebirth, like the dhyānas and the fifty-one mental events, came to be mapped out in scrupulous detail. It may be that this reference to the end of further rebirth from a womb was originally meant to be understood in a general, literary sense, rather than in a technical one. If we wish, we can certainly take this last line as meaning that one does not take rebirth in any form ever again – that one is fully Enlightened. It is hard to be certain either way. What we can be sure of is that it at least expresses complete confidence in the connection between the cultivation of mettā and highly skilful states of mind.

AN INHERITANCE OF JOY
The mettā bhāvanā is not a kindergarten practice.

It is good to contemplate inspiring images of the consummation of mettā, as we struggle to awaken a little of it in meditation. But it may sometimes be more helpful to refer back to the starting point of this whole process of spiritual expansion. The transformation begins with trying to lead a principled and upright human life, and if this preparatory achievement seems a distant goal for most people, clearly it is there that we have to put most emphasis.

We know that an intellectual understanding of selflessness is not enough. But how do we go about integrating that knowledge into a deep and mature emotional awareness? In modern life, especially in the western world, we are not adept at dealing with strong emotion, perhaps especially strong positive emotion. It is therefore not surprising that we underestimate the power of mettā and hence the importance and spiritual status of the mettā bhāvanā. We prefer to equate the goal with a cool appraisal of the true nature of existence rather than with an ardent and un- remitting dedication to bringing all beings into the infinite light and limitless bliss of Nirvāṇa.

Mettā requires strong positive energy. If your positive emotion does not last long in the bright glare of daily life, if you are restless or irritable and unable to be friendly after you have risen from your meditation seat, you will clearly need to go back to the basics of the practice. Before you start meditating, it makes sense to take a good look at how you behave in daily life. I sometimes think that people are not nearly kind enough to one another, either in their actions or in their general attitude. Any unkindness or quarrelling reveals a basic lack of mettā, and unless you are willing to cultivate mettā in your everyday dealings with people there is little point in trying to cultivate it on the meditation cushion. Allowing ourselves to descend into acrimony and rancour displays a fundamental lack of faith in mettā as a path of regular practice. It is as though we leave it in the shrine-room and walk away without it, even though we may have experienced it quite genuinely while there. If that happens, our mettā evidently doesn't have enough strength for it to be carried over into our daily interactions with people.

Mettā is a high ideal, so high that it includes being ready to sacrifice life and limb for others, and it is very difficult to achieve it in its fullness. We must therefore be prepared to appreciate a more limited achievement of mettā as entirely genuine as far as it goes. On the other hand, even our embryonic mettā should not be too delicate. It should be able to survive transplantation, to bloom at least for a few hours in the cold and busy world outside the meditation room. In meditation you may sometimes feel that you are radiating mettā from a safe and rather aloof distance. In that case, you could try introducing a greater sense of imaginative identification with others, as is customary in the karuṇā bhāvanā, for example, in which you aim to feel with others, putting yourself in their shoes. That warmth and empathy should be carried over into your actual relations with people. It might be worth asking yourself whether there is enough warmth in your various relationships, especially with those who also practise the mettā bhāvanā.

The Buddhist path is one of regular steps. The foundation of our practice has to be securely established in mindfulness and mettā before we move on to anything else. For most people, as I hope I have shown, the mettā bhāvanā asks more than enough of their spiritual aspirations, and it hardly needs to be supplemented by anything except the practice of mindfulness. If we are dissatisfied with the mettā bhāvanā, to ask for higher and more advanced practices is self-defeating. Naturally we would like something different for the sheer novelty of it, and we may even persuade ourselves that we are ready for more advanced training. Of course we are in a hurry to move on to the next stage. But all this grasping after the next attainment, the next spiritual goody, is little more than craving and conceit. If we are dissatisfied with the mettā bhāvanā, or if we are not getting on with it very well, it isn't because we have outgrown it, but rather the opposite. It probably means that we have not prepared for the practice adequately, or that we need to be more imaginative, perhaps more intuitive or devotional in our practice. It may just mean that we need to do it for longer periods or more often. The mettā bhāvanā is not a kindergarten practice.

If we follow the path of regular steps, as Buddhists in traditional, pre-modern cultures have done for many hundreds of years, we shall begin by cultivating a happy, healthy, human existence, and we start to practise mettā from that foundation.

These days it is much more likely that we will be on the path of irregular steps. Only once we have learned to meditate do we think of attending to the ethical foundations necessary for successful meditation.

Quite soon we are likely to find that our meditation has ground to a halt, and that we have to start cultivating the essential human qualities of uprightness, amenability, contentment, simplicity, and so on in a more purposeful way before we can make further progress. This happens again and again: you run out of steam and have to retrace your steps to consolidate the ethical basis of your practice. It is difficult to tell which qualities are missing from that basis until you try to build on it and find that it lacks the strength to support you. This is how the path of irregular steps rather haphazardly winds its way.

It is fundamental to Buddhist practice that if you prepare yourself thoroughly, you are already practising. If you have all those positive human qualities, if you are capable, straight, and so on, the chances are that your emotional attitude towards others will already be so healthy and positive as to be akin to mettā. For most people, the task in hand is not chasing after some lofty idea of Insight, but establishing this basis of positive emotion. Without developing love, compassion, faith, joy, delight, rapture, we won't get very far. There has to be a firm, quiet ground of positive emotion to our life all the time. This is well within our reach. It is the normal human state. There is nothing extraordinary, nothing even particularly spiritual about it. We just happen to have sunk below that level, at least for the time being. Thus the way of mettā is not only a path of ever-increasing positive emotion leading to Enlightenment. It is a guide to recovering our basic human inheritance of joy.

NOTES AND REFERENCES

1   Sangharakshita, *Dr Ambedkar's True Greatness*, Triratna Grantha Mala, Pune 1986.

2   Shelley, *A Defense of Poetry*.

3   *Itivuttaka* 27.

4   John MacMurray, *Reason and Emotion*, London 1947, p.19.

5   'Thought', in *Selected Poems*, Penguin, London 1969, p.227.

6   'The Marriage of Heaven and Hell' 67.

7   Saddhatissa translates this word as 'welfare' in later editions.

8   Vinaya, *Mahāvagga* 1.14.

9   Bahiya, *Udāna* 10.

10 Spinoza, *Ethics* III, Proposition 30 (note).

11 Duc de la Rochefoucauld, *Réflexions ou Maximes Morales*, maxim 99.

INDEX

preparation 142
projection 87, 89
prudence 64
Pure Land 138

R
reality 25
reason 16, 85
reassurance 48
rebirth 88, 130, 137, 138
receptivity 70
religion 10, 28, 30ff, 121
renunciation 59, 62
restlessness 48
right livelihood 54,
   see also support, work
rules 67, 70

S
Saddhatissa, H. 21
Śāntideva 102
Śāntināyaka 27, 83
Satipaṭṭhāna Sutta 118
scepticism 69
security 77, 98
self 89, 91ff, 105, 110, 129ff, 133, 134ff,
   see also anattā
self development 135
senses 60
sex 48
Shakespeare, William 105
shame 72
simplicity 46, 53, 58
skill 28
Spinoza 85
spiritual community 78

spiritual friendship 67f, 73, 122,
   see also kalyāṇa mitratā
straightforwardness 42
Stream Entry 131, 137
study 18, 58
suffering *see* dukkha
support (economic) 49, 56
sympathetic joy 19, 116

T
Theravāda 133, 134
Three Jewels 117
Tibet 52
tranquillity 19,
   see also contentment, peace
transformation 96, 102, 122, 139
trust 69, 94

U
unskilful roots 85
unhappiness *see* dukkha
upekkhā *see* equanimity
uprightness 41

V
views 127ff
Visuddhimagga 110

W
wisdom 17, 100, 110
work 51, 54f, 58, *see also* support

Z
Zen 52

WINDHORSE PUBLICATIONS

Windhorse Publications is a Buddhist charitable company based in the UK. We place great emphasis on producing books of high quality that are accessible and relevant to those interested in Buddhism at whatever level. We are the main publisher of the works of Sangharakshita, the founder of the Triratna Buddhist Order and Community. Our books draw on the whole range of the Buddhist tradition, including translations of traditional texts, commentaries, books that make links with contemporary culture and ways of life, biographies of Buddhists, and works on meditation.

As a not-for-profit enterprise, we ensure that all surplus income is invested in new books and improved production methods, to better communicate Buddhism in the 21st century. We welcome donations to help us continue our work – to find out more, go to windhorsepublications.com.

The Windhorse is a mythical animal that flies over the earth carrying on its back three precious jewels, bringing these invaluable gifts to all humanity: the Buddha (the 'awakened one'), his teaching, and the community of all his followers.

Windhorse Publications
169 Mill Road
Cambridge CB1 3AN
UK
info@windhorsepublications.com

Perseus Distribution
210 American Drive
Jackson TN 38301
USA

Windhorse Books
PO Box 574
Newtown NSW 2042
Australia

THE TRIRATNA BUDDHIST COMMUNITY

Windhorse Publications is a part of the Triratna Buddhist Community, which has more than sixty centres on five continents. Through these centres, members of the Triratna Buddhist Order offer classes in meditation and Buddhism, from an introductory to a deeper level of commitment. Members of the Triratna community run retreat centres around the world, and the Karuna Trust, a UK fundraising charity that supports social welfare projects in the slums and villages of South Asia.

Many Triratna centres have residential spiritual communities and ethical Right Livelihood businesses associated with them. Arts activities and body awareness disciplines are encouraged also, as is the development of strong bonds of friendship between people who share the same ideals. In this way Triratna is developing a unique approach to Buddhism, not simply as a set of techniques, but as a creatively directed way of life for people living in the modern world.

If you would like more information about Triratna please visit thebuddhistcentre.com or write to:

London Buddhist Centre
51 Roman Road
London E2 0HU
UK

Aryaloka
14 Heartwood Circle
Newmarket NH 03857
USA

Sydney Buddhist Centre
24 Enmore Road
Sydney NSW 2042
Australia

Buddhist Wisdom in Practice series

The Art of Reflection
by Ratnaguna

It is all too easy either to think obsessively, or to not think enough.
But how do we think usefully? How do we reflect? Like any
art, reflection can be learnt and developed, leading to a deeper
understanding of life and to the fullness of wisdom. *The Art of
Reflection* is a practical guide to reflection as a spiritual practice,
about 'what we think and how we think about it'. It is a book about
contemplation and insight, and reflection as a way to discover the
truth.

*No-one who takes seriously the study and practice of the Dharma should
fail to read this ground-breaking book.* – Sangharakshita, founder of the
Triratna Buddhist Community

ISBN 9781 899579 89 1
£9.99 / $16.95 / €11.95
160 pages

This Being, That Becomes
by Dhivan Thomas Jones

Dhivan Thomas Jones takes us into the heart of the Buddha's
insight that everything arises in dependence on conditions. With
the aid of lucid reflections and exercises he prompts us to explore
how conditionality works in our own lives, and provides a sure
guide to the most essential teaching of Buddhism.

Clearly and intelligently written, this book carries a lot of good advice.
Prof Richard Gombrich, author of *What the Buddha Thought*.

ISBN 9781 899579 90 7
£12.99 / $20.95 / €15.95
216 pages